"There is nothing mor [ ] abused—or more wonderful, powerful, and good—than love. *Love Me Anyway* is a delightful, honest exploration of all the ways we human beings love, brushing away much of the clutter and confusion to explain what it really means to love—and be loved—well."

Karen Swallow Prior, author of *On Reading Well: Finding the Good Life through Great Books*

"C. S. Lewis famously said that if we love anything (or anyone), our hearts will be wrung and possibly even broken. Far from being an easy-breezy, schmoopy, sentimental thing, love is a lifelong battle for those who dare to enter the arena. To love God and neighbor starts with denying ourselves, taking up crosses, and following the One whose own love ultimately cost him his life. Of course, the only alternatives to the costs, inconveniences, and risks of love are isolation and selfishness, which bring the greatest forms of misery. But those who lean into love will find over time that, though it will cost them much, it is also the pathway to great gain. Jared has done a wonderful job spelling this out for us in this wonderful volume."

Scott Sauls, senior pastor of Christ Presbyterian Church and author of several books, including *Jesus Outside the Lines* and *A Gentle Answer*

"Anyone who can write an important book about something this profound while simultaneously making me hum songs from the Bee Gees and Foreigner, well—that guy has my vote. I'm not sure for what. Maybe for everything. Wilson is at his best here. Funny and insightful and kind about the enormously important (and confused) subject of love. The only downside is I had 'I Want to Know What Love Is' going through my head the entire time. I think he planned that, though."

Brant Hansen, radio host and author of
The Truth about Us

"The best writers are faithful stewards of their scars. They craft healing words from wounded pasts. Jared has done just that in this richly textured exploration of love—real love, divine love, the kind that unmakes and remakes us. No one can write a book so honest, so poignant, who has not traveled through the ruins of lost loves and misused loves and come out on the other side radically altered by an encounter with the shockingly gratuitous love of a God who lives to forgive. Jared has. His book is a gift to us all."

Chad Bird, scholar in residence at 1517

"The Beatles and Elvis sang about it. Just about every movie and sitcom cannot have a happy ending without it. Love is at the epicenter of our culture and human identity, but every love song and rom-com falls short when it comes to identity-shaping love. That is the sort of love that can only be seen in God and his gospel. By taking aim at 1 Corinthians 13, Jared shows us the roots of God's love for us through the Scriptures in this very insightful book. This love is the highest good of every human life, and, by the end of this book, you will know the beauty of being loved by God and being a lover of God."

Daniel Ritchie, evangelist, speaker, and
author of *My Affliction for His Glory*

"There are many songs, books, poems, and treatises on love, and Jared Wilson shows us the substance behind all the longings that fill them. This isn't just a book on how to love but how to be loved by the One who, knowing everything, loved us all the way through. Wilson has written a lot of books that I have enjoyed, but this one might be his best."

John Starke, pastor of preaching, Apostles Church in New York City, and author of *The Possibility of Prayer*

"Most of us not only know what love is but think we're pretty good at it. But there are depths and applications of love to be explored—both what it means to be loved and how to love. This book is classic Jared Wilson—thoughtful, creative, biblical, and personal. *Love Me Anyway* will expand the horizons of your heart for what love is all about."

Mark Vroegop, lead pastor of College Park Church and author of *Dark Clouds, Deep Mercy: Discovering the Grace of Lament* and *Weep with Me: How Lament Opens a Door for Racial Reconciliation*

"I consider Jared Wilson to be my generation's Yoda of gospel-centered writing. What drives Jared in this approach to ministry is his personal belief experience with the grace of God and his belief in the gospel of Jesus Christ. In *Love Me Anyway*, Jared explains how this grace impacts every single area of our lives, especially our relationships with others and the church. He draws from a well-known but often misunderstood passage of Scripture to call us to an approach to relationships that can only be understood by the grace of God in our own lives."

Dean Inserra, pastor of City Church in Tallahassee

LOVE
ME
ANY
WAY

LOVE ME ANY WAY

HOW GOD'S PERFECT LOVE FILLS OUR DEEPEST LONGING

JARED C. WILSON

BakerBooks

a division of Baker Publishing Group
Grand Rapids, Michigan

Published by Baker Books
a division of Baker Publishing Group
PO Box 6287, Grand Rapids, MI 49516-6287
www.bakerbooks.com

Printed in the United States of America

Library of Congress Cataloging-in-Publication Data
Names: Wilson, Jared C., 1975– author.
Title: Love me anyway : how God's perfect love fills our deepest longing / Jared C. Wilson.
Description: Grand Rapids, Michigan : Baker Books, a division of Baker Publishing Group, [2021]
Identifiers: LCCN 2021006673 | ISBN 9781540901347 (paperback) | ISBN 9781540901934 (casebound) | ISBN 9781493432905 (ebook)
Subjects: LCSH: God (Christianity)—Love.
Classification: LCC BT140 .W575 2021 | DDC 231/.6—dc23
LC record available at https://lccn.loc.gov/2021006673

Unless otherwise indicated, Scripture quotations are from the Christian Standard Bible®, copyright © 2017 by Holman Bible Publishers. Used by permission. Christian Standard Bible® and CSB® are federally registered trademarks of Holman Bible Publishers.

Scripture quotations labeled ESV are from The Holy Bible, English Standard Version® (ESV®), copyright © 2001 by Crossway, a publishing ministry of Good News Publishers. Used by permission. All rights reserved. ESV Text Edition: 2016

Scripture quotations labeled KJV are from the King James Version of the Bible.

Some details and names have been changed to protect the privacy of individuals.

The author is represented by the literary agency of The Gates Group Agency.

21 22 23 24 25 26 27   7 6 5 4 3 2 1

For
—who else, but the only one?—
Becky Lee,
with all my love,
(such as it is)

Contents

Introduction   13

1. What's Love Got to Do with It?   19

2. Will You Still Love Me Tomorrow?   45

3. Make You Feel My Love   65

4. Love Is a Battlefield   89

5. No Ordinary Love   109

6. True Love Tends to Forget   131

7. Could You Be Loved?   151

8. How Deep Is Your Love?   169

9. When Love Comes to Town   189

10. Now That We've Found Love   209

Conclusion   233

Acknowledgments   237

Notes   239

Introduction

"What is love? Baby, don't hurt me."

Okay, these aren't the most profound lyrics in the history of music, to be sure, but if you can get past the mind-numbing beat and, for a certain generation, the mental image of *Saturday Night Live*'s Roxbury guys bobbing inanely to it, even this vacuous song manages (inadvertently?) to tap into something extremely profound.

Love is the most lauded subject in all of music, all of poetry, all of literature. All of life! It is the thing—if you can call it a thing—we all dream of and live to pursue and, once captured, still wonder at its mercurial feeling. Why doesn't it seem to last once found? Why doesn't romantic love, for instance, continually surge upward into ever-increasing realms of bliss? Why does love so often . . . hurt?

Here's another golden nugget from a hip-hop classic: "Now that we've found love, what are we going to do with it?"

Want more of it, of course. And when what passes for love fails to satisfy the way we expect love should, we assume we're out of love, perhaps were never truly in it. Maybe it's not just ordinary love we need but *true* love. Whatever that is.

"What is love? Baby, don't hurt me" doesn't seem to mean much of anything in the context of Haddaway's dance hit. But it does encapsulate the ancient conundrum of what we imagine love to be. Love is that thing where we never get hurt. Right?

You'd think we'd have figured this out by now, after centuries of enjoying and exploring love. But the songs just keep coming. Because so do the hurts.

C. S. Lewis once said about myth that it was "gleams of celestial strength and beauty falling on a jungle of filth and imbecility."[1] I think love songs are like that. All of these odes to love—from the poetry of the ancients to the bubble-gum romance of 1950s doo-wop, from the moony dreaming of countless ballads to even the raunchy club bangers of today—are feeble grasps at something true, real, satisfying . . . that lies just out of reach. All love songs are gleams of heaven falling on a jungle of imbecility.

So many songs cheapen love. A great many others idolize it. Which is really the same thing. They give us glimpses of love; hazy angles on romance, our heart's desire, the fulfillment of longing, the arrival of a yearned-for peace and joy. But they're still just gleams, never the true light.

As the late, great Larry Norman once sang, "The Beatles said all you need is love, and then they broke up."[2]

Maybe they'd lost that loving feeling.

Maybe you have too. We all lose it from time to time.

One reason we'll always have love songs with us is because we know deep down that love is the greatest thing to ever exist. But did you know the other reason is because love songs are in our DNA?

We have to go all the way back to the first human beings and the first recorded words spoken.

First, there was the divine word of "It is good."

God looked out over his creation, with man and woman as its crown, and saw that it was good "indeed" (Gen. 1:31).

But there was a point where it wasn't quite good enough. Do you remember? It was the time between the creation of man and the creation of woman. God made man, saw that he was alone, and decided that wasn't good (2:18).

And this is where that second word comes in. This is the oldest human utterance:

> And the man said:
> "This one, at last, is bone of my bone
> and flesh of my flesh;
> this one will be called 'woman,'
> for she was taken from man." (v. 23)

You can likely see from the formatting in your Bible that this is Hebrew poetry. This means that the first recorded human words spoken were actually sung. The oldest human words in recorded history were *a love song*.

You can practically hear Etta James's soulful voice sumptuously spilling over the text: "At laaaaast . . ."

"Bone of my bone. Flesh of my flesh."

God ordained marriage then as the only human relationship that can be rightly described as "one flesh." Which is why, forever after, every marriage has been perfectly fulfilling.

Okay, sorry, I know I lost you there. Baby, don't hurt me.

We lost ourselves somewhere, way back there, shortly after this first love song, after this first union and before *re*union was ever a thing, way back in that garden when the first Jerry Maguire declared to the first Dorothy Boyd in that first living room, "You complete me."

Our hearts rose. Our eyes misted. Why? Because we all know the power of "You complete me." We suspect we're worth it. We hear it echoing in the dim memories of the garden we all carry around in our souls. But in the bones and flesh of our reality in exile, after the profession changed, we know that, after all, *it's just a movie.*

These love songs. They're *just songs.*

But what if they aren't?

What if every romantic movie, every romantic song, every insipid Hallmark Christmas show and every flimsy Hallmark Valentine's card, every stupid TV commercial that leverages romance and human fulfillment to sell makeup and blue jeans and bubble gum—even every lustful glance or scroll or click—is not because love isn't out there but rather because somewhere it *is?* As Lewis also said, "If I find in myself a desire which no experience in this world can satisfy, the most probable explanation is that I was made for another world."[3]

And what if, despite our failings and flaws, despite nearly everything we see with our longing eyes and know with our tired minds or even feel with our aching bodies, that other world was actually *here* in some real way?

Would that make your day? At last?

I don't know what has brought you to holding this book in your hands. I don't know if you feel loved right now or if you've ever felt loved, but I'm willing to bet you have at some moment felt unloved. At some point, maybe right now, you've had the nagging thought that love is a myth, a rumor, a haunting.

Maybe love songs make you cry, or make you angry, or make you sick. Maybe love songs feel painful; every time you hear one, it adds insult to your emotional injury.

Have you had love but lost it? Or do you have it, but it's not quite scratching the existential itch you thought it would?

Maybe you've wondered, like I once did, if you could ever be loved. Or if you could ever love in return.

Well, you can. Come walk beside me for a while.

1

What's Love Got to Do with It?

Now these three remain: faith, hope, and love—but the greatest of these is love.

1 Corinthians 13:13

There is no escape from the conclusion that ultimately, love is the only real power.

Peter Kreeft[1]

I fondly remember my first marriage. I remember my feet shuffling nervously on the plywood floor during the wedding ceremony. I wasn't sure if I really wanted to go through with it. The bride seemed equally nervous.

Her name was Elizabeth. She was a pretty girl. Blonde hair, blue eyes. Her father was a dentist, if I recall correctly. So much of that time is hazy to my middle-aged mind today. But I remember the exhilarating flush of young love. The flutter of butterflies in the tummy and the wet spring air on the skin. The world seemed alive with possibilities, a grand stage upon which to carry out the thrills of a whirlwind romance like ours.

My friend Christopher officiated the ceremony. All of our friends had gathered to witness the solemnization of our sacred union in the giant wooden shoe on the playground of the First Baptist School in Brownsville, Texas. We only got thirty minutes for recess, so we had to make quick work of the thing. When it came time to seal the deal, being good Baptist children, we all knew that kissing wasn't appropriate, so I literally kissed a leaf, which Elizabeth then pressed against her cheek. I know, it sounds stupid. And it was. But I vividly recall a year earlier, in kindergarten, another child tattling on me to the teacher for saying the word *lipstick*. And I cried hot little kindergartener tears when I confessed that indeed I had said the word. We were too young to even know real profanity. And here we were acting out one of the most profound human experiences, the event by which a man and woman are covenantally made one flesh. I have no idea whose idea the leaf-kiss thing was, but it seems downright metaphorical to me today. We were hiding our shame with leaves.

The relationship lasted only a few days, which amounts to eons in first-grader years. I don't exactly remember why we played "wedding" that day at recess, but I do remember liking Elizabeth, and I suppose at some point the liking had to be made *official*. In the humid shade of that big shoe, within the sacred trust of all the little rascals, Alfalfa and Darla had to make it real. It's what lovers do. And as silly as that little scene was, I see it now as a kind of epicenter of my lifelong endeavor in thinking about love all out of proportion.

It has taken a lot of years—and a lot of mistakes within those many years—to get closer to figuring out this love thing. I'm still not there, to be honest with you. But I'm about as close as I've ever been, and I hope you won't mind if I share some of that journey with you in this book.

When we're young, of course, we really have no idea what love is. We barely know when we're grown up. But when I was a boy, my innate longing for romance resulted in endless entertainment crushes. I was enamored with Catherine Bach's Daisy Duke and especially Lynda Carter's Wonder Woman. The preadolescent boy's attractions are about who looks pretty and fun.

But my taste in the opposite sex developed. While many boys my age were geeking out about Princess Leia or "Charlie's Angels," or about the Heathers, Thomas or Locklear,

I had more of an inclination toward the "girl next door" types—the Joanie Cunninghams and Mallory Keatons and Carol Seavers.

If you're not getting any of these references, you were likely born before 1960 or after 1990. And if this is the case, you might have missed the greatest television sitcom for the celebration of the best adolescent crush ever: *The Wonder Years*.[2] I was thirteen years old when this show debuted in 1988, and while it technically takes place in the late 1960s, predicated on the adult Kevin Arnold's recollections of his childhood, I felt *The Wonder Years* on a soul level. I still do, in fact.

Winnie Cooper (played by Danica McKellar) was the perfect apex and sum of the entire girl-next-door mythos. But I didn't so much have a crush on Winnie Cooper as I had a crush on Kevin Arnold's having a crush on Winnie Cooper. What I mean is, this show was magically able to tap into the angst and awe of childhood in a note-perfect way and one that reflected my inner life more than anything I'd ever seen. Kevin Arnold was me. No, I didn't have an older brother and sister as he did, and I didn't grow up in the cultural turmoil of the late 1960s and watch neighborhood teenagers graduate into the military draft like he did, and so on, but this temporal context was all beside the point. I felt Kevin's frustrations, knew his social awkwardness, identified with his perennial search for love.

If you followed the show, you know Kevin romanced a few different girls—the bossy Becky (played by McKellar's younger sister, interestingly enough), the exotic Madeline—but beneath and through it all, his heart always beat for Winnie. *The Wonder Years* was about a lot of things, but that's fundamentally what it was really about—an everyboy's love for the girl next door. It was a very specific show about a very universal experience. The show reflected but also transcended its culture in making that romance, with all its pains and all its joys, the constant through line.

So I was gutted, of course, when five years later, after having basically grown up with Kevin, the finale reveals that Kevin doesn't in fact end up with Winnie. Yes, we also learned his father died of a heart attack, and that was sad. But Kevin didn't end up with Winnie! Are you kidding me?

I would reexperience this trauma later with the lesser art of *Dawson's Creek* when, in the series finale, we see that stupid Joey chose stupid Pacey and not her real true love, Dawson. Of course, I was one of only about eight people angry about this outcome, I think. They tried to mitigate the pain of this plot twist by sending Dawson out to Hollywood to become the film director he always dreamed of being, but people with beating hearts like mine know that the whole point in those early *Creek* episodes of the boy watching the entire Spielberg oeuvre in his childhood bedroom wasn't really about watching movies but about the neighbor girl rowing across the creek to climb up the ladder and through his window to watch the movies with him. I mean, she *literally* lived next door.

Get everything material you ever wanted. Accomplish every goal you set. Go every place you ever imagined. In the moments of stillness, when you face yourself, you'll realize that without true love it's all a waste.

What's this all about? I'd be arrogant to think that after thousands of years of human reflection on the mystical gravity of love, I'd be the one to entirely crack the code, but I think that somehow this "crush on the girl next door" stuff has to come from that precious prelapsarian moment when that first man saw that first woman for the first time and couldn't help but sing, "At last!" Romance—and all other longings for relationship, I think—can be traced right back to that garden scene.

But that dreamy moment out of time seemed about as short-lived as first grade recess.

The adolescent boy's attractions begin to churn with lustful undercurrents. That sin has been crouching just outside the door of puberty, waiting to devour him. Everything gets all mixed up. And not just for boys of a certain age but for everyone. We mistake being in lust for being in love. We mistake infatuation for romance. We are messes, so we make everything messy. But deep down, our root desire is really about longing for the experience of real love, that somebody would know us totally and *at the same time* love us completely.

That has to come from somewhere. Sin is disobedience against a holy God, but it is also misdirected attempts at getting from someplace else in some other way what God himself gives and in his very self actually is. As Bruce Marshall once wrote, "The young man who rings the bell at the brothel is unconsciously looking for God."[3]

The Book of Love

The doo-wop group The Monotones was the first to wonder, wonder, who, bad-doo-oo-hoo, who wrote the book of love. For their part, Frankie Lymon and the Teenagers wondered why fools fall in love. Songs like these speak to the seemingly uncrackable cipher of love. No animal instinct can explain it. No pragmatism can solve it. It's the stuff of potions and angels and Mr. Sandman. The most popular songs of the 1950s were much, much simpler than the pop songs of the late 2000s, but they also wrestled with love in a way these later songs rarely do. Pop music, like a boy, grows up, and lust ends up poisoning the whole enterprise.

On the way to the coffee shop to write this chapter, I was listening to some old love songs on the radio and realized most of them wouldn't rate today, and not just because the music style is out of fashion. When our forebears sang about love, they stood in awe—both of the objects of their desire and of love itself. Sure, they're praising external appearances a lot of the time, but like the ancient poets, they're comparing eyes, hair, and smiles to heavenly beings, ethereal feelings, and the like. They are reveling in beauty and, as it always does, true beauty transports them, connects them to an ecstasy beyond what is merely seen. "Are the stars out tonight?" The singer can't tell, because his love has arrested his attention with her loveliness. He only has eyes for her.

Fast-forward to today's fixation on faceless bodies, the comparison of women's private parts to dump trucks and milkshakes. The poetry is gone. We've lost that lovin' feeling.

I know I sound like a grumpy old man right now. And it's not fair to compare the best examples of musical yesteryear with the worst examples of today. There are some good songwriters out there still wrestling with the mysteries of love and saying some profound things. But in terms of popular music, mainstream songs ostensibly about love have gotten cruder, ruder, and, indeed, less poetic. Our culture does not speak of love in lovely ways.

It may surprise some to know, however, that this is not because as a people we are more sinful today than anybody else was in the past. We may have grown coarser, but it's only because we have gotten collectively tired of holding up the pretense that we are good people. There may yet be a revival of virtue and propriety—cultures do tend to swing like a pendulum from extreme to extreme—but we'll still be just as sinful even when we recover our shame.

This cycle has played out from the beginning of time. The broken love of Genesis 3 spills quickly into the first murder. The wickedness intensifies then, calcifying in the earliest culture. It's not long, historically speaking, before God pours out his wrath on everyone in the world, minus one family with which he means to reboot humanity. But even that reboot does not proceed sinlessly. Drunkenness, bloodthirsty violence, and sexual immorality reemerge into the world almost as soon as that family steps back onto dry land.

The question of where love comes from—Who wrote the book on it? Why do fools fall into it?—*is* this story. It's the same story of sinful, broken people navigating a sinful, broken world. The best love songs, then, even if written by godless heathens, still somehow manage to point to the peace and joy of unbrokenness, to the shalom of love fully known and realized. "I don't know if we're in a garden or on a crowded avenue," sang The Flamingos, who only have eyes for you; and they have, perhaps unwittingly, managed to summarize the civilizational progression of love itself. For we began in a garden and now find ourselves exiled on the avenue—crowded physically and mentally and emotionally—and still longing to return to that garden, where our eyes may be filled with the glory of love.

Every love song is a gleam of beauty falling on a jungle of imbecility. The gleams tell us there is a brighter light out there, a glory more glorious than even the glory of earthly loves. There is a story that makes sense of all the stories, even the terrible ones.

This story begins in the eternal mind of the Author. And it makes perfect sense that the greatest romance ever told would come from the God who is love in his very self. "God is love," the apostle John tells us (1 John 4:8, 16). It's not just that he's loving, though he certainly is. And it's not just that he *has* love, though he certainly does. No, John boldly asserts that God's very self is the very thing all humankind has always been starving for and searching for. Your constant need for love is fundamentally a constant need for God.

Now, how is it that God can be love in his very self? Some dullards have said that God made humankind because he was lonely, because in effect he needed someone to love. However, this would make God not God at all but more of a glorified proto-man. It was Adam whose solitude was not good; it was Adam who was perfected by receiving one to love and to love him in return. God did not become love upon his creation of anyone or anything. He *is* love. Which means he's always been love.

But if there was a time before anything else was, yet there's never been a time when God was not, how can this be? Love needs an object, doesn't it? You can't love *nothing*.

Our knowledge of God helps us here. What do we know about the one true God? We know that he exists eternally in three persons. There are not three gods; nor is there one god who sometimes manifests in one of three different personalities. Rather, God is a Trinity of equally and essentially divine persons. *This* is how God is love. He has always had love within himself, enjoying the relational love among the trinitarian fellowship. The Father loves the Son, and the Son loves the Father. The Father loves the Spirit, and the Spirit loves the Father. The Son loves the Spirit, and the Spirit loves the Son.

If we find love mysterious, is it any wonder? The very fountain of love, he who is love in his very self, is an eternal and inscrutable wonder. Have you figured out the math of how the Trinity "works"? Well, then, neither can you figure out the math of how love works.

The love of God is so intense, so perfect, and the glorious love each person of the Triune Godhead gives to the others becomes the basis for expansion of this love outside of the impassible reality of itself. God doesn't need anyone else to love, and he certainly doesn't need to receive love, but he sovereignly wills to make creatures in his own image, to know his love and to love him in return, to reflect his own glory in a special way.

So when that first naked guy stood there looking at that first naked gal, and they both lacked shame, and they both felt nothing but the ineffable quality of love—so ecstatic and glorifying that the only reasonable response was to sing— they were experiencing something of the intratrinitarian love of God.

It lasts for about a minute. Eventually that man and woman decide something else may satisfy. They don't want to just know God but be in his place. The perfect experience of love is shattered. And this is still at the beginning of the Book!

But the sordid history book about love-hungry sinners reaches its climax when the Word becomes flesh. Love puts skin on. He is the new Adam—sinless and able to give love perfectly. Jesus says a lot about love, but he mostly just *does it*. He loves anyone and everyone. The people you expect he should. And the people you suspect he wouldn't. Even some people you think he *shouldn't*. He appears to love willy-nilly. He's not asking anyone's permission. He just loves freely, widely, promiscuously.

Jesus loves all the wrong people. People who can offer him nothing. People who cannot love him the way he loves them. People who hate him. He doesn't seem hindered at all by their lovelessness or their unloveliness. He loves them so much, in fact, that he very often puts himself in their position, stooping to their level, touching their wounds, embracing their pain. He ends up loving so much that he takes their shame upon himself, even their sin and the condemnation it deserves. He loves all the way to the cross. And as the most popular Bible verse in the history of the world tells us, "For God loved the world in this way: He gave his one and only Son, so that everyone who believes in him will not perish but have eternal life" (John 3:16).

There is no greater love than this (15:13).

So now you know who wrote the book of love. The only one who could. God created this crazy little thing called love as a reflection of himself and of the story of the gospel—the good news of the radical love of God through Jesus Christ, whose sinless life, sacrificial death, and glorious resurrection

save sinners who repent of their sin and tru'
gospel helps us crack the code.

And now you know why fools fall in love. ᴅᴜᴄᴄ
sinners who don't know God or want anything to do with
his love have been made in God's image. The reflection of
Love is in their bones. Love, though corrupted because of sin
and distorted because of the fall, is in every person's DNA.

It's for this reason that so much of what we consider love
becomes not-love so easily. Sin is why we don't always feel the
love we want and more often don't give the love we should.
But the Book tells us something vitally important about that
mess too.

I Want to Know What Love Is

The Bible nowhere offers a direct definition of *love*. It often
describes different kinds of love, but it never offers the kind
of summation we find in a dictionary. So how do we know
what we're even talking about when we talk about love? I
think, based on everything the Bible does say about love,
in all its shades and meanings, we might define love this
way: *love is an orientation toward others for their glory
and for their good.* This refers exclusively to interpersonal
love, of course, not to lesser "loves" like your love of kit-
tens, French fries, that song or that movie, or your favorite
football team.

Let me unpack this definition a bit. Love can and often
does come with certain feelings we call love. We might prop-
erly call these *affections.* You can have these in different ca-
pacities and intensities for a significant other or for your
children or for your parents or for friends. I feel and exhibit

loving affections for all kinds of people. But what I feel for my wife is different, of course, than what I feel for my best male friends.

We feel certain things about those with whom we're close or to whom we're otherwise connected. But we also feel certain things about inanimate objects or even persons we don't know. The feelings are not as strong, of course, or as enduring, but sometimes we do not have loving affections for our spouse either, or our friends. We can be angry with them. Or we may just be struggling at certain moments or in certain seasons to feel the way we used to feel or think we ought.

Does this mean, then, that we have stopped loving them? Or should stop loving them?

The world very often says yes. This is why fools who fall in love are said to have fallen *out*. When you're not in love anymore, it's time to find a new love.

Obviously, our definition of real love must transcend feelings. What remains when certain loving feelings are hard to come by? That's when real love kicks in. Because if love is going to be genuine, it must reflect our immovable God (who is neither moved nor changed by feelings) and the constant love he has within himself and for others. This means love must exist beyond how it makes us feel. The love the Trinity enjoys is the love of mutual glorification, a love that is simply because the Trinity *is*. In other words, the Father doesn't love the Son because of the Son's performance or the reciprocity of love. The Father loves the Son because he's the Son. He loves the Son as the Son is, because of who the Son is, because *he* is the Son.

Do you see the significance yet for the love you and I have for each other?

If I truly love you, it will not be because you perform a certain way for me—that you "do something for me," in other words. That would not be love at all. If I truly love you, I will love you because you are you. That is real love of you rather than what you do or how you make me feel. And that's how love is an orientation toward others for their glory. It aims to delight in the them-ness of persons. I affirm the image of God in you by loving you simply for being you. Really, I'm affirming the glory of God to have made you and to be showing something of himself in and through you.

I can do this whether or not you even believe there is a God. Also, to be oriented toward you for your glory doesn't mean I affirm everything you think, say, or do. It doesn't mean I affirm your desires or appetites. If you are engaged in something that demeans or otherwise serves to obscure the image of God in which you are made, you are diminishing your own glory. It would be unloving, then, to agree with you about something with which God disagrees.

Love is not an all-approving grin. It seeks not the other person's pleasure or agreement but the other person's *glory*.

Similarly, love is an orientation toward others for their good. This means when I love you, I want what is truly best for you. The Bible is quite good at helping us understand how so many pleasures we pursue are violations of God's holiness and therefore destructive to our very selves. We may not think so or, if we do, even care. But not everything we want to do, say, or think is good. Therefore, if I love you, I will only support or affirm what is genuinely for your good. This is why in Romans 12:9, the apostle Paul connects genuine love to detesting evil and clinging to what is good. Love is an orientation toward others for their glory and for their good.

Okay, so how do we do this? What does real love look like?

Paul gives us a stunning picture in perhaps the second most famous Scripture passage in the history of the world.

Higher Love

We've all heard 1 Corinthians 13 recited at wedding after wedding. This biblical chapter on love is to weddings what "Amazing Grace" is to funerals. Which is to say, even people who don't know God or profess faith in Jesus, when they want their wedding ceremonies to have a whiff of religion in them, go to 1 Corinthians 13.

You've no doubt heard the passage read at many weddings in front of couples who honestly have no idea what they're doing. The words feel gushy and mushy and light and fluffy, and they really have no clue what love is going to require of them. It sounds like uplifting religious poetry to their ears, when really it's a call to die.

I officiated a few weddings in my time as a pastor, and I think pastors at these shindigs should spend a considerable amount of time just asking, "Are you sure? But are you sure? Like, are you really *sure*?"

In his book *What Did You Expect?*—which is a great title for a marriage book, by the way—Paul Tripp writes:

> I performed the marriage, so I got the call. It is almost always made by the wife, and she is calling because she has actually been forced to face what, somewhere in the recesses of her mind, she knew to be true—she and her husband are

sinners. The call is usually made a few days or weeks after the honeymoon. On the honeymoon the self-orientation of sin is overshadowed by exotic cuisine and gorgeous sites, but when the couple returns to real, everyday life, minus these distractions, they are forced to face who they really are and what their marriage is actually about. . . .

Sara called me at 6:30 AM the day after the ceremony. I picked up the phone to these two words: "It's over!" I knew it wasn't over. In fact, I was happy that she was making the call so soon. I thought Sara and Ben were the smart kids in the class. They had gotten to the end of themselves quickly.[4]

The invitation to love is an invitation to die to yourself and live for the good of others.

And this kind of love has to do with so much more than marriage. The gospel of Jesus Christ's love affects all of our relationships—or it *ought* to. And when you do relationships with anyone for any length of time, you see that you can't *not* be in a relationship with a sinner. Of course, neither can they.

So the invitation to love is also an invitation to subdue our baser instincts and embody the love from on high, the love that came down to us, for us. Real love is love that resembles Jesus.

When the grace of God changes a sinner, it can't help but overflow out of that person and extend to others. And redeemed sinners find more and more that they can conduct themselves in all of their relationships through the powerful love of God. And when you do relationships through the love of God, you learn over and over again that love has a lot less to do with feelings and a lot more to do with forgiveness.

Real love, as God intends it, is meant both as a gift to be enjoyed and as a glory to be reflected on his Son.

Let's refamiliarize ourselves with the passage, how about?

If I speak human or angelic tongues but do not have love, I am a noisy gong or a clanging cymbal. If I have the gift of prophecy and understand all mysteries and all knowledge, and if I have all faith so that I can move mountains but do not have love, I am nothing. And if I give away all my possessions, and if I give over my body in order to boast but do not have love, I gain nothing.

Love is patient, love is kind. Love does not envy, is not boastful, is not arrogant, is not rude, is not self-seeking, is not irritable, and does not keep a record of wrongs. Love finds no joy in unrighteousness but rejoices in the truth. It bears all things, believes all things, hopes all things, endures all things.

Love never ends. But as for prophecies, they will come to an end; as for tongues, they will cease; as for knowledge, it will come to an end. For we know in part, and we prophesy in part, but when the perfect comes, the partial will come to an end. When I was a child, I spoke like a child, I thought like a child, I reasoned like a child. When I became a man, I put aside childish things. For now we see only a reflection as in a mirror, but then face to face. Now I know in part, but then I will know fully, as I am fully known. Now these three remain: faith, hope, and love—but the greatest of these is love. (1 Cor. 13)

Paul is writing these beautiful things to a very ugly church. The Corinthians are fractured by division and fraught with immorality. They are spiritually weak and very, very immature. So in the first twelve chapters of 1 Corinthians, he's reminding them of the gospel and then working through various theological and practical issues. He addresses their division, he teaches them about wisdom, he rebukes their immorality, he instructs them on church discipline, and he talks about lawsuits and marriage and divorce and Christian liberty and spiritual gifts. And then at the end of chapter 12 he talks about the unique nature of the church body, which then gives way to this beautiful passage on love.

All the stuff that came before, he's saying, must culminate in love.

The form of 1 Corinthians 13 is really interesting too. Paul places his description of love (found in vv. 4–6) between two interesting theological bookends. Each bookend clarifies the *why* of love and really the *what* of love. The first bookend (vv. 1–3) is Paul's way of culminating everything he's said to the Corinthian church thus far (chapters 1–12) with what matters most. He's saying that even if you get chapters 1–12 right—your behavior is well-managed, your worship is orderly, and the like—if your heart isn't tuned to the music of the gospel, it will all be wasted. We know who real Christians are, Jesus says in John 13:35, because of what? Their love.

Love is, in fact, the highest good.

This is what Paul is getting at in that first theological bookend. The person who possesses a supernatural ability to speak in tongues, an exhaustive knowledge of the Scriptures, or any other miraculous religious power who doesn't also possess love effectively has nothing.

This is what Paul is getting at in that second theological bookend too. In verse 13, he writes, "Now these three remain:

faith, hope, and love—but the greatest of these is love." As it pertains to virtues, love is the end-all, be-all.

Why?

Perhaps because it emanates from God himself, the One who is love. Perhaps because God has no faith or hope. He is the proper object of those two virtues but has no need to exhibit them himself. But love? He certainly has love within himself.

There are other reasons why love is "the greatest," and I'll explore a few of them later, but here we see how the two theological bookends of 1 Corinthians 13 establish love as the highest and greatest virtue.

Only true love can get us through those "day after the ceremony" moments. Only true love can get us through any moment when we feel as though most certainly "it's over."

Loving feelings can get you through a wedding ceremony and a few days, weeks, maybe even a few years. But only the highest love can get you through the lowest moments. The absence of the highest love makes the richest person the poorest, while the presence of it makes the poorest the richest.

The Glory of Love

Love is the highest good. And by "good," I mean both virtue and possession. Love is the highest virtue, adorning and grounding every other virtue—peace, contentment, joy, even moral purity—in the essence of God's character. And love is the greatest possession. You know this. You feel this. It's why you can achieve and accumulate—you can get pleasure and money and stuff—but it all feels empty when you don't feel loved or have someone to love.

We feel empty when we don't feel loved by our parents or by our siblings or by anybody else. Our friends. Even our church. But it's not just our feelings that are hindered by lovelessness. Our very survival may be threatened. For example, multiple studies have shown the physiological impact on infants in orphanages whose basic needs for nutrition and hygiene are provided for but who otherwise are not touched, held, or spoken to.

> For instance, in Romania in the 1980s, by ages six to 12, levels of the stress hormone cortisol were still much higher in children who had lived in orphanages for more than eight months than in those who were adopted at or before the age of four months, according to a study from Development and Psychopathology. Other work has shown that children who experienced early deprivation also had different levels of oxytocin and vasopressin (hormones that have been linked to emotion and social bonding), despite having had an average of three years in a family home.[5]

In the end, you can certainly live without love, but without love, you may not want to. The impact of lovelessness is huge, almost incalculable.

Why?

Because real love is, in part, an implicit affirmation of the glory of the *imago Dei*—the image of God—in us.

"If I have the gift of prophecy and understand all mysteries and all knowledge," Paul writes, "and if I have all faith so that I can move mountains but do not have love, I am nothing" (1 Cor. 13:2). It doesn't matter if you're the smartest person in the room. If you know the most Bible verses.

If you've served in church the longest. If you give the most money. If you read the most books. If you behave the most morally. These are all lesser glories. They do not reflect the glory of the image of God like love does.

Love is the most glorious glory. This is because, when given to others, love gives people a glimpse of God's love for them. Love for others becomes a living apologetic for the existence of the God who is love. And love is the most glorious glory because, when given to God, love gives him his due, agreeing with him about his own worthiness and preciousness.

You may wonder at this point how my definition of love fits with our consideration of love for God. What does love seeking the glory and the good of others have to do with God? The glory part we get. Loving God glorifies him, gives him through our worship the praise and honor he deserves. But what about his good? Can we "do good" to God?

God, of course, lacks for nothing. He does not need anything from us, as if he is somehow deficient without our contribution, whether a good work or a good word. We certainly cannot do the opposite of good to God in the sense that we cannot harm him or diminish him in any way. He is God.

But we can harm his reputation. We can diminish others' sense of his worthiness with our lovelessness. When we love God, we do good to him by magnifying him and commending him to our neighbors.

And there is still another way we, in effect, "do good to God" by our love. See, the Son of God so identifies with the poor, the persecuted, and the sick that when we care for them, he receives it not simply as a love to them but a love to himself (Matt. 25:40). When we don't forgive others,

God takes it personally (6:15). John connects love for God's children with love for God as well (1 John 5:2).

One may argue these Scriptures refer only to our love for Christian brothers and sisters, but the author of Hebrews connects care for the stranger with caring for the Lord's servants too (13:2). And in any event, Jesus makes it clear both that everyone is our neighbor and that love for neighbor is inextricable from love for God. Thus, when we do good to others, including those who don't like or who aren't like us, we are doing good to him by magnifying his love, which is glorious and gracious.

I have a friend named Mez who grew up in a painful world as an unbeliever, as one who in fact hated both God and people who claimed to speak for God.

Mez's grandmother was a prostitute. His grandfather committed suicide. His mother ran away with the best man at her wedding. And his father was an alcoholic and a gambling addict. At two years old, Mez was abandoned on the street. Between ages two and fourteen, he was shuffled around between thirty and forty institutions, orphanages, and foster homes. By age twelve, Mez was doing drugs. By age sixteen, he was homeless.

When Mez was homeless and dealing drugs, he encountered a group of young men at a community center who had come there to play soccer and to share the good news about Jesus. He utterly despised them and their message, rejecting the ideas of God's wrath for his sin and God's love for his salvation with equal disgust for each. He constantly insulted the young men and threatened them.

By age twenty-one, Mez was incarcerated in a maximum security prison. Those Christians he'd spent so much time hating came to visit him. They persisted in love even while he persisted in hate.

Mez said, "Upon my release on parole, one of the Christian men whose face I used to spit in gave me a place to live. He gave me a home that I could call my own."[6] Eventually, the love he was shown, even in the face of his hateful rejection, began to open his heart to hear the gospel, and Mez was converted. Today, Mez is a missionary and pastor, a church planter in his native Scotland, where he also runs an organization dedicated to planting gospel-centered churches in the poorest neighborhoods. He is where he is today certainly because of God, and because God saw fit to use Christians who never stopped loving even when they were hated.

That Mez is a lover of God today is itself an incredible story of astounding grace. And it's a testimony to the glory of love.

This is what Paul is describing in 1 Corinthians 13 between those two bookends. For love to be glorious, it must be a radical reorientation of our selves for the glory and good of others. Those evangelists endured Mez's abuse in order to be *for* Mez's glory and good. If we want to know love for ourselves, it begins with this emptying of self and choosing of the other. This is the way of transformation. This is the way to glory.

Of course, I didn't know any of this during my short-lived first marriage. Lasting all of thirty minutes and beginning in a big wooden shoe should've been just two indications that love was only being played with, *playacted*. And yet, it still took me a very long time, well into adulthood in fact, to learn how to stop playing with love, to stop acting. I wish I'd outgrown the lesser glories that harmed others, myself, and my relationship with God much, much earlier. The people I've hurt certainly do too.

But the most remarkable thing I've learned in all my failures, in all my stupid spitting on love, my fist-shaking at love, is that real love never walked away. I came to my senses one night in the loneliness of our guest bedroom, feeling like death in the ruins I'd made of my life. I was a wretched tangle of sin and despair. But I discovered that night that, when I was at my worst, love never left. In fact, I've learned that love was made just for such needy moments.

2

Will You Still Love Me Tomorrow?

Love is patient.

1 Corinthians 13:4

There is nothing as impenetrable as true patience.

St. John Chrysostom[1]

I sat on the edge of the bed, my head in my hands, tears pooling in my palms. My mother sat next to me, hand on my back, consoling. I was in junior high school, and I'd just had my heart broken. Again.

Why didn't the girls I liked ever like me back? What was wrong with me?

Would I ever know love?

It seems a bit silly now to an adult heart to consider the threat of inconsolable loneliness to a lovelorn teenager. In the grand scheme of things, I was thinking way too big about something objectively small. But it didn't feel small then. And the root affections weren't small then—and they aren't small now. We were made to be loved. We just weren't made to bring a junior high–level of thinking to it.

We call these experiences "young love," but it's really just young. It's immature, and not just because it's the stock-in-trade of young wannabe Romeos like me but because it's an underdeveloped form of attraction, a remedial kind of love. It's not exclusive to the adolescent. A lot of us grown-ups still mistake self-interested infatuation for love.

Because love is an orientation toward others for their glory and for their good, love doesn't despair when it isn't reciprocated. Love isn't self-seeking (1 Cor. 13:5).

The truth is, I don't even remember the name of that girl I was *so in love* with! I can't even picture her face. This tells me something now that didn't register back then. It tells me that I was more in love with the idea of love than I was in love with what's-her-name.

I remember I'd had a crush on this girl in our church youth group for a while, and my impression was that even in our relatively small class, she had no idea I existed. The crush became crushing one evening at a youth fellowship event. I remember we were playing volleyball. A new guy had shown up, some kid who had just moved to town. He wore a cool Vuarnet T-shirt and impeccably rolled jeans. His hair was slick with mousse. What a jerk. And what I remember was that this girl did not hide at all that she was immediately interested in him.

You don't even know him! I said to her in my mind.

But she didn't know me either. And, of course, I didn't know her. I suppose I was just infatuated with the idea of her.

In the ridiculous movie *Win a Date with Tad Hamilton!*, a Piggly Wiggly clerk named Rosalee wins the contest that promises a romantic rendezvous with her celebrity crush. But the ensuing relationship with her new movie star boyfriend begins to wake her up. The titular Tad just sees her as another advantage to his personal journey, if not as the antidote to his waning career. When Rosalee realizes the celebrity who has been romancing her is really a superficial flirt simply using her to feel good about himself, she says, "You don't love me, Tad. You just love the idea of me."[2]

It's the truth. And in the end, she winds up (of course) with the boy next door who actually knows her and loves her *for her*.

I did not learn the lesson so neatly as presented in ninety minutes of Hollywood fluff. My own heartbreak played out a few more times through my teenage years. I don't remember most of those girls' names either.

What's any of this got to do with patience? Well, when we love the *idea* of someone more than his or her actual person, we are really just in love with ourselves—in love with the image of the relationship we entertain in our own mind or in love with simply how they make us feel. This is vain love. We may think we're adoring them, but really we're just worshiping ourselves. And you and I make fickle gods. We get testy. We grow impatient. We become despondent, self-pitying. Real love is twisted and corrupted by impatient lovers.

There are woefully few love songs celebrating the virtue of patience. But there are so many opportunities for true love in the midst of agonizing waits. Think of the prodigal son's father. How painful must that have been, hoping against hope his son would return while carrying the hurt of having been wished dead (which is what asking for your inheritance early means) and the dread of whatever his wayward son might have been doing out in the wild world.

And then the son returns; there is no hint of frustration, of resentment—at least, not from his father. No, the man rushes out to meet his son and throws a party. For as long as he was not appreciated nor even loved himself, the father still waited patiently. That's love.

Pastor and author Zack Eswine once said that Christians are addicted to doing big things famously as quickly as possible when Christian ministry is mainly doing small, overlooked things over a long period of time.[3] The growth of the kingdom, even our own growth in the Christian life, necessitates an extraordinary patience that is constantly at odds with the way of the world, as well as the inner disposition of our flesh. This makes our impatience, naturally, a kind of failure to love.

If love is an orientation toward others for their good and glory, impatience is an orientation toward the self for our satisfaction and convenience. The impatient person can't even be rightly said to love themselves, because in the long run, impatience does not serve our own good or glory.

Nearly all of us have trouble waiting for comforts and conveniences. We want what we want *now*. But some of us right now—and all of us at some point—will have trouble waiting for things far more important. Reconciliation, maybe. The alleviation of anxiety. The return of a prodigal child or a prodigal parent or a prodigal spouse. Maybe you've been waiting a long time for healing from sickness or disability. And, of course, we all wait for that blessed day when pain, grief, and even death will be no more.

But maybe the hardest thing to wait for—because we just know deep down that it will heal all that seriously ails us, even perhaps make other persistent ailments much more bearable—is love itself.

Are you growing impatient? Are you waiting for love lovelessly?

Have you been waiting a long time for someone to love you back? Maybe it's a wandering child or a neglectful sibling. Maybe it's a wayward friend. I know a lot of pastors who are waiting for their churches to love them back. Maybe you've got your eye on a potential significant other who's not giving you the time of day. Maybe the person who continues to consume your love without returning the favor is actually your spouse.

Maybe you're not sure how long you can keep going. Remember that love is patient. True love will, in fact, be painfully patient.

You Can't Hurry Love

I don't remember exactly what words my mother said to me in the wake of my junior high heartbreak, but that bedside consolation is burned into my heart. I know she didn't tell me not to be sad. She didn't tell me I was being silly. She *did* say something about there being other girls out there. The words didn't stick, really, because logic can't assail lovesickness. But she was beside me, feeling my pain. And that helped.

Love is patient, because love gives people space to be themselves. If you love someone, you give them room to breathe.

My wife and I are very different. I'm an introvert; she's a walking party. I tend to process my thoughts and feelings internally; she uses all the words for all the things. She likes to plant flowers and tool around in the yard; I'm an avid indoorsman. We have a lot of similar tastes that make time together a lot of fun, but we will likely never approach problems, questions, or challenges with the same processes or even the same instincts.

In the beginning of our marriage, as in the beginning of most marriages, we looked to each other to complete ourselves. "You make me very happy" so easily becomes "You exist to make me happy." Little frustrations can erupt into enduring resentments when expectations aren't met. In the beginning, I wanted my wife to be more like me. Why? Because I really love myself. I think I'm great. And all the things about her that aren't like me seemed like deficiencies.

But when a man loves a woman, he wants her to be—and I'm sorry for sounding a little Osteeny here—the best version of herself she can be. Love wants the beloved to flourish. It exists for the glory and the good of the other. This means that even if I don't "get" why my wife is wired a certain way, I acknowledge that her difference from me is not a deficiency, and, in fact, I'm not even loving God if I think of her that way, since he's the one who made her the way she is.

Obviously, sin complicates this whole affair. All of our wiring is impacted by indwelling sin, the inward bent of the flesh. God didn't make *that*. But our uniqueness—our idiosyncrasies, the ineffable quiddity of our fearful, wonderful selves—this is all God's doing.

To place the expectation upon her, then, that she must more resemble me in order to be loved by me is an attitude of passive hatred. Patience in this case is about trusting that God knows what he's doing in making people so different. Impatience with the differences of others is how we say to God that he screwed up.

But it's not just with others' quirks and traits that love calls us to be patient. We are also to be patient with their failings, even their sin. This patience is not excuse-making permissiveness. It is more like a hopeful long-suffering. Love hopes all things, after all, and endures all things (1 Cor. 13:7). We do not have to tolerate sin that endangers us or others. Patience doesn't mean we never address wrongdoing. It just means we don't stop loving. (Indeed, very often confronting wrongdoing is the loving thing.)

Knowing that we ourselves are all-day, everyday sinners about whom the Lord never throws in the towel should help us in our consideration of the garden-variety sins of our loved ones. Patience with sinners is how we show we haven't forgotten God's patience with us.

I Don't Want to Wait in Vain for Your Love

An older friend of mine told me a story once about having cheated on his wife with a secretary at his workplace. He'd committed this sin more than thirty years ago. Eventually, he'd broken off the relationship and broken free from the behavior, but he never told his wife. For over three decades, then, he lived with the guilt and shame of this secret.

Finally, one night as he and his wife of over forty years were preparing for bed, he realized he couldn't hold the secret in any longer. He hoped that so much time had passed that it would seem a lesser offense than if it had happened "yesterday." But he also knew that such a revelation would be extremely painful to his wife, no matter how long ago it had been. He wasn't sure how she was going to react. But he had to tell her. So he did.

She slowly turned and looked at him. And then she said something that completely took him by surprise. She said, "You idiot. You didn't think I knew about that?"

He froze. She knew? All along, she knew? Flustered, he searched for words. He suddenly felt even more guilty, even more ashamed. She'd known about his sin all these decades. Finally, he worked up the courage to say, "Will you forgive me?"

She looked at him and said, "You idiot. Do you think if I hadn't forgiven you that I'd be in this bed with you right now?"

My friend had been walking for thirty years in a forgiveness he didn't even know he had. And this woman had been patiently enduring his secrecy for thirty years. Surely, she had borne the pain of this betrayal for a long time. What she did is not necessarily prescriptive for everyone. But still she exhibited an extraordinary patience in daily forgiving her husband even the sin he wouldn't confess.

Consider the patience of Christ who, as his wrists strained against the nails hammered through them, looked down through blood and tears to say about his tormentors, "Father, forgive them, because they do not know what they are doing" (Luke 23:34).

This was the most urgent moment of all. Heaven and hell hung in the balance. And even through blinding agony, Jesus asked the Father to give his murderers just a little more time.

Love is patient.

How patient? Consider those closest friends of Jesus. These twelve men received the best seminary education and discipleship program a Christian could get. They walked up close and personal with the Lord of the universe for three straight years. They were daily witnesses to his grace and wisdom. And at the end of the journey, they still didn't quite get it. Peter heard all of Jesus's words about how the kingdom of God comes and what must take place, and still he was lopping off an ear to protect Jesus one minute and denying him the next.

The other disciples are not much better at loving Jesus. But at no point does Jesus say to them, "You know what? I thought you were better than this. I've had it with you." I'll say more about the remarkable relationship between Jesus and his closest friends in chapter 9, but for now it's enough to say that obviously our Lord loves with an extreme patience.

In his *Works of Love*, Søren Kierkegaard writes,

Christ's love for Peter was so boundless that in loving Peter he accomplished loving the person one sees. He did not say,

"Peter must change first and become another man before I can love him again." No, just the opposite, he said, "Peter is Peter, and I love him; love, if anything, will help him to become another man."[4]

What the philosopher illustrates here could be summarized this way: *the grace that loves us as we are can also empower us to be what we ought.* The Bible speaks of God's grace that way. Grace is the gift of Christ himself through his sinless life, sacrificial death, and glorious resurrection. This gift covers our sins—pardons them, then forgets them. But the same grace that justifies us also sanctifies us. It is the grace of God that, beyond our conversion, gradually conforms us to the image of Christ (2 Cor. 3:18; Titus 2:11–12). Kierkegaard is saying that Christ's love in the gospel of grace met the sinful Peter where he was but also carried him further along the road to becoming his true self.

My friend Ray Ortlund uses this formula to describe the same concept in a church setting: Gospel + Safety + Time. What he means is, people in church communities need regular exposure to the message of grace in order to grow spiritually. But if our church communities are not safe places for sinners—not safe places for *sin* but for sinners—to confess, to be honest, to *be themselves*, we can quench the work of grace in their lives. Indeed, to place expectations, explicit or implicit, upon people that they must play a religious role, pretend to be totally put together, or otherwise constantly "measure up," we unsay with our community what we claim to believe about grace. So people need regular exposure to the gospel, the safety to actually know and be known by others, and then they just need time. They need the space to not have it all figured out instantly. Discipleship cannot be microwaved. Everybody we meet, whether in our church or in our neighborhood or in our living room, needs our patience. That's what love looks like. You can't rush it.

How does this relate to loving one's enemy? Well, one reason we even have enemies is self-centered impatience, whether ours or theirs. Someone hasn't granted the other the space to be human or the grace to be forgiven. We want our enemy to change. How do we manage that? Jesus did not say to berate them. He did not say to cajole them. He did not say to manipulate them. What did he say?

True Love Ways

That same Peter who failed Jesus more than a million times comes to his Teacher with a pressing question:

> Then Peter approached him and asked, "Lord, how many times must I forgive my brother or sister who sins against me? As many as seven times?"
>
> "I tell you, not as many as seven," Jesus replied, "but seventy times seven." (Matt. 18:21–22)

I don't know if Peter got his calculator out or what. If you're a literalist, you are obligated to forgive an offense against you just 490 times, and then you're off the hook. But this is one of the times Jesus is not being literal. "Seventy times seven" is a symbolic reference to completion. In this instance, it basically means this: "As many times as it takes."

But what if the person never repents?

Jesus could very well be saying to Peter that he is to forgive someone who sins against him *forever.*

Is he crazy? Sometimes we read things like this in the Gospels and our first inclination is to figure out how it doesn't really mean what it obviously says. Jesus in the Sermon on the Mount says to turn the other cheek when someone strikes you, and we instantly start going into all the exceptions Jesus "clearly" had in mind but didn't say. He says if someone commands we go with him one mile, we are to go with him two, and we immediately assume Jesus didn't mean just anyone but people we might actually enjoy walking with for a while. We don't take Jesus seriously. We don't consider him "street-smart," savvy about the way the world "really works."

But Jesus's commands reorder our priorities, our allegiances, and our perceptions. He is constantly demanding that everyone center on him rather than themselves. This entails a radical reordering of our perception of our enemy. Jesus says to "love your enemies" (5:44), not just because that's what he does in dying for rebellious sinners but because love humanizes them. To love someone is to refuse to objectify them or to turn them into a monster or a soulless force in our minds. Christ demands we take our enemies out of the category of object and return them to the category of image-bearer—even if they refuse to do the same for us!

To love your enemy requires seeing your enemy as a human being who is imperfect like you—indeed, who is a sinner like you. So loving your enemy requires tremendous patience. Jesus goes further to say we are to pray for them (v. 44). Why? I think because prayer is how we acknowledge that God is in control, that his ways are higher than ours, and that we are submitting to the better desire of our enemy's good and glory rather than their downfall or shame.

Prayer is the spiritual discipline of showing patience with God himself too. It's how we acknowledge that God knows what he's doing even in providentially directing jerks and meanies into our lives. And it's how we surrender to him our inclination toward vengeance. When we love those who hate us and pray for those who persecute us, we are in spirit handing them over to God, hoping not just that they will get what they deserve but that, like us, *they won't.* We are patient with God's timing, as he may plan to turn them around eventually—and he may intend to use us to do it!

Think of the child who, in a fit of frustrated rage, says to her mother, "I hate you!"

The mother is obviously hurt, struck to her very heart. But fighting back tears, she doesn't say, "Sometimes I hate you too!" or "You don't know the half of it!" Instead, she says, "Well, you may hate me, but I love you. And nothing will change that." It's not true to say that what the child says or does doesn't hurt. But the love will not be changed. If anything, the love may become even more lavish, more furiously defiant to match the rage. If a child's hate will be turned to love, only love will do the trick. But if our giving of love is contingent upon reciprocity, we will be sunk.

Here's how Kierkegaard addresses this situation:

> If when another says, "I cannot love you any longer" one proudly answers, "Then I can also get along without loving you."—Is this independence? Alas, it is dependence, for whether he shall continue to love or not is dependent on whether the other will love. But he who answers, "Then I

will still continue to love you nevertheless"—his love is made eternally free in blessed independence.[5]

And now we are approaching the biblical concept of true love. Love doesn't stop when it isn't returned. Love is not based on merit.

Kierkegaard calls this "blessed independence," but it's really not independent at all. As it pertains to human-to-human relationships, the experience of one-way love can be a very lonely thing. This is why it is only enduringly possible when it is dependent on the one-way love of God.

As God loves us unconditionally—purely out of the Love he himself is—we receive the boundless supply we need to love others in a similar way. (I say *similar* rather than *same* because we are finite creatures still beset by sin and the flesh. We cannot replicate God's perfect love. But we can be filled with it and bear witness to it.) We can love others regardless of their response to or acceptance of it by remembering God's grace for us.

Loving someone who doesn't love you back is how you know your love is true.

Love Will Keep Us Together

The consistent picture throughout the Scriptures of the highest form of love is a self-giving love that endures. In the Old Testament, the Hebrew word for this love is *hesedh*, which according to scholar Leon Morris has almost no obvious English equivalent.[6] The closest we may come to explaining *hesedh* is "steadfast love" (or "steadfast devotion"). This word is used 245 times in the Hebrew Scriptures, and it is almost always ascribed to God's disposition toward his people. It is also tightly connected to the concept of covenant.

A covenant is like a contract in that in it two parties mutually agree to a relationship based on certain provisions. But a covenant is unlike a contract in that when someone breaks a contract, the contract itself ceases to be binding. A contract, as in business arrangements, is based on a default distrust. One party may decide not to hold the other party liable for breaking the contract, but the broken contract effectively ends the relationship. Not so a covenant.

A covenant can be broken, of course, but because it is based on a default trust—a proactive commitment—a broken covenant does not necessarily end a relationship. It can. But that is not an absolute consequence. One party can still maintain the covenant by upholding his or her side of it.

So what we see throughout the Old Testament narrative is largely a picture of sinners breaking covenant with God but God persisting in his love for them. That's covenantal love. That's *hesedh*. One side fails and fails and fails, and the other side loves and loves and loves.

The New Testament corollary is the Greek word *agape*, which Morris says is "a love given quite irrespective of merit, and it is a love that seeks to give."[7] This kind of love is sacrificial, one-directional, and gracious.

What's fascinating about the word *agape* is that it is not used very frequently in Greek literature before the New Testament. But suddenly the Holy Spirit is inspiring those writers to use *agape* left and right. It was not a new word, to be clear, but the early Christians, because of the apostolic teaching in the Scriptures, gave it a newness. As with the word *gospel* (*evangelion*), which at first held the cultural connotation of a king's herald delivering news, perhaps like a town crier, Christians hijacked *agape* and infused it with the meaning of grace. *Agape* is a sacrificial love, a love that gives of itself even to the point of death for the good and glory of the one being loved.

Hesedh in the Old Testament and *agape* in the New are the deepest forms of love and run parallel to each other, as both reflect a one-way covenantal commitment from one person to another. One person may not feel that love or return that love, but *hesedh* and *agape* are not contingent upon that. They love simply to love. They love for the good and glory of another. This is, of course, how God loves us. He needs nothing from us. He is not thrown off by our failure or discouraged by our puny affections for him. He loves because he is love, and he loves those who do not love him back.

The *hesedh* of God is why we have the *agape* of the cross.

In a way, you could say these kinds of love persist in steadfast devotion because they are driven by the glory of love itself. They don't see what they stand to gain, only what they delight to give. This is the only way to explain how God never forsakes his people and how he would even send his own Son to die for reprobates.

Hesedh and *agape* are the loves that have seen it all and aren't going anywhere. They are the loves that persist in the face of hardship, suffering, shattered expectations, muted affections, and, yes, even hatred. *Hesedh* and *agape* are what 1 Corinthians 13 is all about, which is why so many married couples that break up should really think about what they were doing when they had it recited at their weddings.

Hesedh and *agape* are how marriages can survive the breaking of a covenant. A beleaguered husband or an exhausted wife can, in the face of human uncertainty and a dismal return on their investment, nevertheless keep the covenant, knowing Christ is keeping his. It doesn't mean they always have to. I know Christians differ historically on the sensitive subject of divorce, but I do believe the Bible provides some specific allowable grounds for it. So Christians suffering from a broken marriage covenant don't always have to keep it. But *hesedh* and *agape* mean they *can*.

These loves keep forgiving, not seven times but seventy times seven. These loves keep loving, come hell or high water.

Obviously this requires a deep well of patience. To love someone who doesn't love you back especially requires a long-suffering commitment to love for the sake of love. Only a love driven by the grace of God in Jesus could manage such a feat, all by the power of the Spirit. It costs too much to accomplish apart from his compensation. It hurts too much to accomplish without his consolation. It takes too long to accomplish without his patience.

Loving someone who doesn't love you back is hard. But it's how we learn if we really love them or just the idea of them, what they do for us, or how they make us feel. And the joy of it is, so many times, as one lover painstakingly loves day in and day out, hoping and praying and desiring the good of the other, exhibiting a supernatural level of patience, that love finally takes over. One day the beloved wakes up and realizes that the love available that day must really be love, simply because it is actually there today and not just yesterday.

For past-tense love to be trusted, it must be present.

And for the lover, almost nothing can draw us closer to knowing the love of God than the hardship of being unloved by others. It is a bitter truth, but I'm here to shoot you straight. Unrequited love is sanctifying. Or it can be, provided we press into the love of Christ, who never leaves the bedside of our brokenness, his hand on our back, consoling us with his own tender patience.

3

Make You Feel My Love

Love is kind.

1 Corinthians 13:4

Only as we drink down the kindness of the heart of Christ will we leave in our wake, everywhere we go, the aroma of heaven.

Dane Ortlund[1]

I was a sixteen-year-old kid browsing the florist shop for a gift for my girlfriend. A hopeless romantic and a creative type, I specialized in unique gifts and poetic letters, but everybody knows sometimes the old standbys are standbys for a reason. Girls love flowers.

I'd noticed an older guy, probably in his midthirties, shuffling nervously around the shop since I got there. After I selected a bouquet for my sweetheart, I paused at the counter to compose some lovey-dovey lines on a card. My fellow browser approached me. "Hey," he said.

I looked up at him. "Yeah?"

He held up a bouquet of six red roses. "Do you think my wife would like this?"

I paused for a moment. How would I know what his wife would like? I didn't know her. "I don't know," I said. "Do you think she would?"

He looked at the bouquet then, as if the flowers might answer him. "I think so," he said. "I just don't know."

Then I noticed he held a greeting card in his other hand. He kind of waved it at me. "Look," he said, "could you help me?"

I'd really rather not, I thought. "Help you with what?" I asked.

He then proceeded to tell me a terrible story about his wife being in the hospital. "Cancer," he said. I don't remember if he told me what kind. But he said she'd just had some kind of procedure and was about to come home, and he wanted to do something nice for her.

Immediately I softened toward him. And it felt very strange. I was a sixteen-year-old kid, and this thirtysomething stranger was asking me for advice. I suddenly felt like I was his buddy, maybe even his pastor. And then he asked me for something that stopped me cold. "Could you tell me what to write in here?"

He meant the card. I was astounded. What kind of husband didn't know what to write to his sick wife? What kind of man didn't know how to say something romantic to the woman he loved? I couldn't believe it.

But I helped him. As he procured a pen and unfolded the card on the florist's counter, he waited dutifully to take dictation from my poetic tongue.

"I don't know," I said. "Tell her you love her. Tell her that no matter what she's going through, you'll always be there for her."

I'll never forget what he said next. He kind of chuckled and said, "Well, let's not get crazy."

In the span of that three-second statement I suddenly felt like I had a very deep insight into his relationship. I was angry with him, I confess. I was picturing his cancer-stricken wife back at the hospital hurting, afraid, probably lonely. And her husband was hitting up a high school kid for words of comfort he should have found easily in his own heart. I wasn't going to be his Cyrano. "Well," I said, "at least tell her you love her." I quickly paid for my flowers and hustled out.

In the last twenty-five years I've thought of that unpoetic stranger a handful of times, mostly when I've bought my wife a card for her birthday or Valentine's Day and been stumped as to what to write in it. Turns out, deep thoughts of love don't always come easily. In fact, the deeper and more substantial the relationship, the harder they come. Shallow relationships are made for fluffy words. But relationships that matter? That last? That mean something beyond infatuation and fun? Even the wisest among us will fumble for the right thing to say.

The Bible's philosopher puts it this way:

> Three things are too wondrous for me;
> four I can't understand:
> the way of an eagle in the sky,
> the way of a snake on a rock,
> the way of a ship at sea,
> and the way of a man with a young woman. (Prov.
> 30:18–19)

The bottom line? We pretty much stink at love. Whether by our inability or our unwillingness, our fallenness just fouls everything up.

Tainted Love

It was the worst of times, it was *the absolute worst* of times. It was the age of sound-bite wisdom, it was the age of clickbait foolishness, it was the epoch of blind belief, it was the epoch of virtuous incredulity, it was the season of blight, it was the season of spiritual darkness, it was the winter of despair all summer long. We had everything before us, we had nothing before us. It was 2020. (I pray Charles Dickens will forgive me.)

By the time you read this I also pray it's all in the rearview mirror. COVID-19 anxiety. Political hostility. Cultural chaos. Racial divisions. Church divisions. Injustice and incivility. I hope it all feels like a fever dream, something we can't quite believe really happened. But I suspect we'll be in this mess for quite some time.

As someone who has spent a great deal of time on social media since the rise of blogging nearly twenty years ago, I have watched the rise and fall of internet empires and the coming and going of internet trolls, but something feels different about the last few years. For one thing, we no longer regard angry people online as some kind of aberration. Anger is becoming more and more the norm. It's become even a virtue. It almost doesn't matter what side of an issue you take; the shrillest voices rise to the top. We used to ignore them. Now we reward them.

We used to have to go searching if we wanted to feed ourselves on loud, narrow-minded pontificating. Now it finds us. It's on every cable news station, in every social media stream, and very frequently in our pulpits or sitting next to us in Sunday school. We value it so much, we elect it for public office and fly its flag and then plead for it to deliver us from itself. Our favored politicians and favorite pundits become avatars of our own dysfunctions.

The dumpster fire year of 2020 hasn't so much caused this phenomenon as it has revealed it. What we are inside gets turned outside when difficulty hits. When we're stressed, afraid, or otherwise afflicted, who we really are gets revealed. And we've seen a lot of true colors in 2020.

Recently a guy driving a car with a "Coexist" bumper sticker flipped me the bird, and I thought, *Well, that's about right.*

My wife has renounced Facebook entirely because of the toll taken by daily watching relatives and friends being awful to each other.

We should not be surprised, actually, that the world runs this way. Those who do not know Jesus have no centering hope. Even the idols of peace or happiness can't deliver us from the bent of our flesh. But when we regularly see those who claim to follow Jesus, who claim to have made his way their way, acting just like the world, it should stop us in our tracks and make us ask, "Why?"

I come from a church culture that has made opposition to worldliness a staple of its preaching. Our stances on things like fornication, adultery, pornography, and homosexuality are unambiguous. We warn regularly against the church's being influenced by these immoralities. But somewhere along the way, many of us forgot there are multiple ways to be worldly. This is what Paul writes in 1 Corinthians 6:9–10:

> Don't you know that the unrighteous will not inherit God's kingdom? Do not be deceived: No sexually immoral people, idolaters, adulterers, or males who have sex with males, no thieves, greedy people, drunkards, verbally abusive people, or swindlers will inherit God's kingdom.

What an interesting list! Those who will not inherit God's kingdom practice the kinds of sins we expect: idolatry, adultery, homosexuality, theft, and drunkenness. But Paul also includes "verbally abusive people" in this warning.

Verbally abusive people are engaging in a damnable worldliness.

We have lost the virtue of kindness. We even despise it and those who practice it. We consider them not really street-smart or not in tune with the dire need of the day, which is apparently to match anger with anger and hatred with hatred. We consider kindness weak, old-fashioned, sinfully effeminate.

Where is this coming from?

The reason beleaguered husbands are intimidated by romance and social media trolls dehumanize their opponents is the same: our need for and to love is compromised by unkindness.

This dysfunction has been in us since the fall of humanity, since the very moment we turned away from God's goodness and into ourselves and thus lost appropriate wonder of him and his image-bearers. Adam was supposed to protect Eve, but when he got called on the carpet, he sold her out. He blamed her for his own sin. (And she in turn blamed the devil for hers.) We've been "othering" each other ever since. We deflect, shame, and scapegoat.

We know how to please ourselves, because that's where our affections naturally go. None of us really stinks at loving *ourselves*.

This is the same reason why, even when we do love someone, we struggle to show it. We think, *Well, they know*. But we never expect others to assume the same about us. We want them to *actually love us*, not just take us for granted.

In my time as a pastor, I saw this play out in countless marriage relationships, as wives desperately wanted their husbands to say they loved them, to pray with them, to demonstrate even some minor overtures of romance, while husbands fully aware of these desires still struggled with apathy about them. And in my time as a husband, I've seen it play out in my own marriage.

Why is it so hard to give someone the love we know they need?

Jonathan Edwards describes our trouble with the cumbersome weight of love this way:

> In this world the saints find much to hinder them in this respect. They have a great deal of dullness and heaviness. They carry about with them a heavy-molded body—a clod of earth—a mass of flesh and blood that is not fitted to be the organ for a soul inflamed with high exercises of divine love; but which is found a great clog and hindrance to the spirit, so that they cannot express their love to God as they would, and cannot be so active and lively in it as they desire. Often they fain would fly, but they are held down as with a dead weight upon their wings. Fain would they be active, and mount up, as a flame of fire, but they find themselves, as it were, hampered and chained down, so that they cannot do as their love inclines them to do. Love disposes them to burst forth in praise, but their tongues are not obedient; they want words to express the ardency of darkness (Job 37:19); and often, for want of expressions, they are forced to content themselves with groanings that cannot be uttered (Rom. 8:26).[2]

What is mainly in view here is the trouble we have expressing our love for God. But the root problem is the same as the trouble we have expressing love for our neighbor, whether it's the person next door or the person next to us in bed. There is a "great clog and hindrance to the spirit." We are "held down as with a dead weight." We know we ought to express our affections, but we find that we can't. Why?

Edwards attributes it to our fleshliness. We carry around loving hearts in "clods of earth." The apostle Paul described the tension in Romans 7, where he is just plumb fed up with his inability to do what he knows he ought to do.

We were made to reflect heaven, to live in heavenly ways, but our fallenness ties us to this earth. To use Edwards's language, our fallenness keeps us from flying.

This is why it's hard sometimes to say "I love you." This is why it's hard sometimes to actually love the people we say "I love you" to.

It's not simply sin, though that is our biggest and primary problem. We all fall short of God's glory that way; we are bent inward and corrupted with a besetting rebellion. But we also suffer the effects of sin that we may not directly be guilty of. We are frail. We get tired. We suffer hurts and bear scars.

Think of a woman who desperately wants to fulfill her husband's sexual needs but finds herself stifled for reasons she can't explain. Her heart wants to, but her body won't cooperate. Is she in willful sin of sexual neglect? Maybe. Perhaps sometimes. But for a great many spouses in this situation, the sexual frustration is the result of an ambiguous shame. Maybe it's the result of anxiety. Maybe it's the result of years of a church discipleship that taught only the "dangers of sex," trafficking in a shame and fear that frustrates even marital sexuality. Maybe it's the result of her husband's insufficient efforts to meet her needs. Maybe it's the result of years of sexual or other physical abuse. Sometimes we struggle to love others not because of our sin but because of someone else's, because of the terror of trauma that has effectively rewired our instincts, dulled our pleasures, eroded our trust and sense of freedom. This, too, is carrying a "dullness and heaviness."

But there's another way the struggle sometimes is made manifest. I think of the way we all tend to wield our own needs against each other, turning the desire for love into demands for appeasement. Willard Harley first published his bestselling book *His Needs, Her Needs* in 1986. It has since gone on to sell over two million copies. The gist of the book is fairly helpful. Husbands and wives (tend to) have different ways of feeling loved. Whether we ought to call them "needs" or not is somewhat of a pedantic argument, so I will set that aside for a moment. The bottom line for Harley is that understanding each other's specific needs is an important key to loving each other and building a happy marriage. Author Gary Chapman covers similar ground in his book *The 5 Love Languages*, which has now become a cottage industry unto itself. The breakdown in our relationships occurs, according to these thinkers, when we seek only to have our own needs met or to try loving someone according to our own "language." We get frustrated when the thing that works for us doesn't work for another. It is easier, more natural, to love according to our own needs and our own unique wiring than it is according to someone else's.

These books have become sore spots in the consciousness of the evangelical subculture today because of their misuse. We insist others love us according to our needs and our language, which is directly against the spirit of love to begin with. Love is not self-seeking (1 Cor. 13:5).

We stink at love.

But we have to press forward anyway. We have to love anyway. We really do have to obey the command to love. We really do show we are Jesus's followers in the way we love each other. It's that important.

That guy in the flower shop just needed to suck it up and put some words down, however pathetic. It wasn't going to sound like Shakespeare, but the harder it would be to compose, the more loving it would be to present to his wife. The only way to get past the flesh that fails us is to crucify it. This might mean not waiting for someone to meet our needs before we seek to meet theirs. It might mean learning to speak someone's love language even if they're not fluent in ours.

It might mean giving what meager strength or intellect you have for the good and glory of another. It often means accepting someone's meager efforts, because your love isn't contingent upon their performance. A loving husband or wife who is struggling with sex doesn't discount how comforting it may be to their spouse. And a loving spouse isn't pressuring or shaming their partner for being a troubled soul in a broken body. This is what it looks like for two fallen creatures to show kindness to each other. This is true love.

Think of what love might result if we all put each other's interests ahead of our own. We'd find ourselves in a beautiful stalemate.

None of this works so long as our love exists purely as a feeling, purely as an idea, an abstraction. We ought never neglect the affections, which include the feeling of love. But love that *only* feels isn't real love.

For love to be kind, it must move.

Love Me Do

You might wonder what frustrated romantics and Twitter trolls really have to do with each other. Here's the answer:

both claim the intention of love without the action of it. With the former, it sounds like this: "Do I really need to do all this mushy stuff? She knows I love her." With the latter, it sounds like this: "I am harsh *because* I love."

There is certainly a way love is tough. There is certainly a way it can be harsh. I'll talk about that in a later chapter. But the gaslighting taking place even among professing Christians online over their slander, ridicule, and harassment of others is downright satanic. It is an inversion of vice into virtue. I can actively hate you, but if I claim it's for your good—or for the good of the church or some tribal movement within the church—I think I can call it love and get away with it. None of these folks ever seem to ask themselves, *If I was treated this way, would I feel loved?*

And the answer is "Of course not."

We have a word for people who constantly hurt others and say it's because they love them: *abusers.*

I thought a lot about this perversion of love during 2020. I've seen people I love decide love looks like hate. Something that seems so obvious a reversal to me doesn't appear obvious to them at all. I've been slandered, harassed, and mocked for not "getting it." I do confess that the rise of socially acceptable hatred among Christians has taken me by surprise. But while I admit I don't know the Bible as well as I ought to, I nevertheless don't quite see the emphasis that others do on treating our neighbors like dirt.

I've watched as church members run off faithful pastors, as pastors run over people on social media, and as Christians of all kinds have determined that people *not their kind* are responsible for everything wrong in the world.

Why are we doing this? A few reasons, I think.

Fear drives all manner of sinful thoughts and words. And we are living in a great season of fear. Between a global pandemic, lawlessness in the streets, hurricanes and wildfires, and ongoing political tensions, we've got lots of fuel for fear. And fearful people are constantly insecure and thus constantly defensive—and thus constantly lashing out.

Obviously, hatred is also an extreme anger. The wrong kind of fear leads to the wrong kind of anger. We think we're being righteously indignant or prophetically courageous when really we're being judgmental and quarrelsome. When we're angry about perceived wrongs or injustices, we tend to look for a scapegoat. We look for someone to blame, someone to take it out on. Anger must have an object.

Finally, some people just feel lost. They feel out of control or out of their depth. They're confused, and confusion fuels both fear and anger. We don't have all the answers, and we're finding it increasingly difficult to navigate chaotic times when all the experts seem to disagree so often with each other. We're uncomfortable with *not knowing,* so we create theories that explain "what's really going on" and accuse others of conspiring against us. Our lack of clarity must be someone's fault.

Maybe hatred is the result of all of those things—or none of them. But I doubt I'm the only Christian who's noticed we're in a pronounced season of tearing down. And I doubt I'm the only one growing weary of it.

Certainly there is a time, as Ecclesiastes 3:3 tells us, to tear down. There is wide application of that. Some institutions or structures may have reached their time of replacement. That kind of tearing down is a kind of laying to rest. Wickedness and injustice should always be torn down. That kind of tearing down is a kind of righteous rebellion. Sin should be rebuked, false teaching refuted. But if you're always in tearing down mode, you end up tearing down more than you ought.

There's a lot falling apart these days. But I think Christians ought to be especially interested in *building up*. Sure, you could spend all your free time arguing with people online and otherwise grumbling about them in your heart, but you could also consider how constantly being set to attack mode conflicts with the fruit of the Spirit. As Paul says, "'Everything is permissible,' but not everything is beneficial. 'Everything is permissible,' but not everything builds up. No one is to seek his own good, but the good of the other person" (1 Cor. 10:23–24).

I think many of us have lost this inclination, this fine art of edification—the art of building each other up—and it's high time to recover it. Indeed, it is an urgent need of the day.

It is not enough to claim love. It is not enough even to genuinely feel love. Without works our faith is dead (James 2:17), and this is true also for love. "Action follows affection," wrote the Puritan Richard Sibbes.[3] Or, if you prefer, it was dc Talk who said, "Luv is a verb."

Love seeks the good and glory of another. The glory we seek in another is the kind that helps them experience freedom in Christ, enjoy the grace of God, and know the security of being loved despite their sin or struggles. Edification is work that serves those ends. It seeks to lift someone up.

What does it look like?

I think it begins with prayer. It's very difficult to hate someone you're interceding for. Anger leads us to dehumanize, to objectify our enemies. But bringing them before God in prayer is our way of acknowledging his image in them and submitting our will about them to him. The genuinely prayerful heart has no room for bile. Further, prayer is how we acknowledge our own powerlessness. In prayer we are admitting the love we are commanded to give can only come from God himself. If not for him, we would not be able to love (1 John 4:19).

Secondly, edification looks like encouragement! Not withering sarcasm, not relentless nitpicking, and certainly not angry accusations. There are no Bible verses that command us to suspect, accuse, scrutinize, or attack one another. But there are plenty that call for encouraging one another. Honest question: Do you think American Christians in particular are known by our encouragement of one another? And yet we have clear commands to that end. Christ gave the watching world the right to judge our orthodoxy in at least one respect—our love (John 13:35). And Paul writes, "Therefore encourage one another and build each other up as you are already doing" (1 Thess. 5:11).

In prayer, we are submitting our concerns and others' good to Jesus. In the act of encouragement, we are commending the way of Jesus, who came not to condemn but to save. So the most important thing we can do to show someone we love them is point them to Jesus! We "meet one another," as Dietrich Bonhoeffer says, "as bringers of the message of salvation."[4] Helping people see Jesus is how we make sure we worship him and not ourselves. It is hard for people to see Jesus in us when we're hurling insults at them.

Oh, I know, Jesus hurled insults too. But that wasn't his normal course of ministry. It's another bizarre perversion that so many believers jump over large swaths of biblical exhortation to love and kindness in order to make their life verse that one time Jesus cleansed the temple.

I have even noticed the startling irony of people on social media arguing all the livelong day about "getting back to the gospel" who never seem to articulate anything approximating the gospel. If your demeanor in the public square gives the impression of an impossibly angry judge or trigger-happy accuser, how do you expect to commend the gracious Christ?

Committing unrelenting attacks on the brethren, railing against the vulgarities of the world while remaining silent about the vulgarities of our own favorite leaders, and daily maintaining a snide and scoffing spirit all give the impression of Jesus as one who is petty and cruel and harsh. What if instead—just hear me out—we spent at least as much time (if not more) positively magnifying the grace of the gospel and the beauty of Christ?

It's not too late to change. We don't have to keep following these clods of dirt down the chaotic spiral of fear, anger, and confusion. We don't have to keep tearing each other up. Sure, that may be good for views and clicks. And it's easier than kindness. But hatred is how the world works. The spirit of the age is all about biting and devouring. You and I are different. Aren't we?

In Ephesians 4:32, Paul writes, "And be kind and compassionate to one another, forgiving one another, just as God also forgave you in Christ." In Titus 3:2, he tells us "to slander no one, to avoid fighting, and to be kind, always showing gentleness to all people."

I don't know, but these seem unequivocal to me.

Paul is, of course, only drawing from Jesus's words to the disciples: "I give you a new command: Love one another.

Just as I have loved you, you are also to love one another"
(John 13:34).

Followers of Jesus are to love each other the way Jesus has
loved us. Now, how does Jesus love us?

Certainly Jesus is stern with us sometimes. He disciplines
those he loves (Heb. 12:6). But does he shame us? Does he ridicule us? Does he nag us or nitpick us or harass us or harangue
us? Undeniably, no. His yoke is easy and his burden is light.

Jesus comes as an emissary of kindness to us. As Love
embodied, he is the very portrait of mercy and gentleness
and self-control. He is a lion for us but a lamb *to* us. He does
not lord our failings over us or remind us of our sins. He is
our Prince of Peace.

If you simply want to be heard or feared or catered to, by
all means, forget kindness. But if you desire the good and
glory of others—if you love people—you will remember
what grace Christ was and is for you, and you'll extend that
to them. That's what love does. It builds up (1 Cor. 8:1).

Love Me Tender

In the 2002 film *Punch-Drunk Love*, Adam Sandler plays
Barry Egan, a troubled man afflicted by loneliness and rage.[5]
He is frequently overwhelmed and desperate to feel normal.
Barry is likely on the autism spectrum, though that is never
explicitly stated. But he is slow to register social cues and is
insecure around people in general, fixates on certain routines
and habits (he obsessively buys hundreds of cases of a particular brand of pudding because of an air miles promotion
they are running), and lives constantly in a depressive state
over his inability to fit in.

One of the most heartbreaking scenes in the entire film is when Barry makes an awkward, anguished appeal to his brother-in-law for some psychological advice.

"I wanted to ask you something because you're a doctor," he says. "I don't like myself sometimes. Can you help me?"

"Barry," his brother-in-law says, "I'm a dentist."

It's a little bit funny, but it's not played for laughs at all. In fact, the first time I saw this scene, I couldn't help but tear up. Barry is desperate for help. He's tired of being who he is and doesn't know how to stop. It's a very vulnerable moment, because it takes place at a family get-together where it is made obvious that Barry's four sisters hate him. They ridicule him and tease him. Overcome with emotion he doesn't know what to do with, he smashes the sliding glass door to the kitchen. He has no idea how to process the pain he feels. He is broken.

Barry says to his brother-in-law, "I don't know if there is anything wrong with me because I don't know how others are."

That line feels so truthful. It's delivered so meekly, so helplessly, it struck me in my heart. I have felt like Barry before. Lonely. Misunderstood. Unable to cope with thoughts and feelings I don't understand myself.

But then something happens. It's a movie, of course, so that something is a woman. Her name is Lena (portrayed by Emily Watson). And Lena is weird and awkward too. So for a while she's not put off by Barry's weirdness. They are two broken people who have found each other.

One of the most brilliant sequences in the movie is a montage depicting their blossoming romance set to Shelley Duvall (as *Popeye*'s Olive Oyl) singing "He Loves Me." The camera swoons. Director Paul Thomas Anderson utilizes an array of colors in dazzling fashion. The lovebirds have found a kaleidoscopic escape from the darkness of life apart. Their awkward love becomes a means of power to overcome their frailty.

Later, in a climactic showdown with a bully, Barry says to him, with a different kind of anger than before, "I have a love in my life. It makes me stronger than anything you can imagine."

Barry didn't need tough love. He didn't need a pep talk. He needed someone to enter into his brokenness with him and love him where he was. Loving him where he was gave him the power to get out.

The opening sequence of the movie is a very confusing one. It shows Barry going about his morning in the nondescript warehouse where he works. Suddenly a truck crashes violently on the street outside, flipping over multiple times. At the same moment, seemingly unrelated except by timing, a cab screeches to a halt at the curb, and someone in it drops a harmonium on the sidewalk before it tears back off down the road.

Barry is perplexed. He seems scared of the instrument at first, or at least scared of being accused of stealing it. But eventually he snatches up the harmonium and hustles it into the warehouse, where he hides it in his office.

He tries to play it, but the instrument is broken. Something inside doesn't work. He fiddles around with the bellows, tinkers around with the keys. It will make noise but it is discordant, off-putting.

The harmonium is Barry himself. And as the movie progresses, as Lena's love begins to work a healing power in him, he slowly repairs the instrument. By the end, he is playing the harmonium, and his tune is in sync with the movie's score. What has happened? Love has breathed new life into him. He has a purpose, a sense of settledness about himself and his own place in the world. This is what love can do. As Jennifer Warren and Joe Cocker sang, "Love lifts us up where we belong."

This is what love can do if we will be intentional and merciful in it for others.

Kindness can fix us.

This is what God's loving-kindness has done for us. Jesus comes near to us, even putting on the frailty of our flesh. Though without sin in himself, he was willing to endure all the sin and shame this broken world had to offer. He wasn't put off by our ugliness. He wasn't run off by our rage. He wasn't repelled by our rebellion. He conquered it all with his powerful, gentle love. "The LORD is near the brokenhearted" (Ps. 34:18). "He heals the brokenhearted and bandages their wounds" (147:3).

And by coming near and bearing our burdens, by taking our sin to the cross and leaving it dead in the grave, by rising victoriously to defeat death and the powers of evil, he redeems us, resurrects us. He breathes new life into us. His love soothes our pain, binds our wounds, and sets our brokenness. In him, we become more ourselves. Before we were just pale imitations. But now we are in tune with the music of heaven.

And here is the great inversion knowing Christ makes: we stop excusing our hatred as love or calling our vices virtues. We stop dismissing our own sin while reveling in the shame of others'. As St. John Chrysostom puts it,

Love changes the nature of things and presents herself with all blessings in her hands, gentler than any mother, wealthier than any queen, and makes difficulties light and easy, causing even our virtues to seem facile, and vice itself becomes very bitter to us.[6]

It is the kindness of Jesus in his gospel that enables and empowers us to be kind to others. We don't have to manipulate or maneuver. We don't have to ridicule and revile. We can lean into the Lord's tender embrace. We can find safety there. He meets us where we are.

As Lord of heaven, Jesus brings the reality of heaven with him wherever he goes. Heaven is the place where everything is in perfect alignment with the reign of God. This is why we pray God's will be done on earth "as it is in heaven." It is the one place unstained by the fall. So when Jesus heals blindness or leprosy, it is to be seen as a picture of the perfect peace of heaven. When Jesus multiples loaves and fish or turns water into wine, it is to be seen as the perfect abundance of heaven. And when Jesus touches a bleeding woman or gathers little children into his lap or washes his disciples' feet, it is to be seen as the perfect tenderness of heaven. These are signposts to the place where kindness reigns, because Jesus does.

How we treat others is a signpost to where our hearts reside. We are bearing witness with our words and deeds to where we are going. Do we spread the aroma of heaven? Or of hell?

The kindness of God has a profound effect on how we see others. Or it should. If we know we are secure in Christ, we won't be driven by fear, anger, or confusion toward others. We don't need to have control over them. We won't see them as impediments to our own happiness or well-being. Not because people never do anything wrong or never deserve anything bad but because *so do we*, and yet Christ still covers us with his grace.

> Therefore, as God's chosen ones, holy and dearly loved, put on compassion, kindness, humility, gentleness, and patience, bearing with one another and forgiving one another if anyone has a grievance against another. Just as the Lord has forgiven you, so you are also to forgive. Above all, put on love, which is the perfect bond of unity. (Col. 3:12–14)

Are you impatient with the faults of others? Do you hate their sin more than your own? Do you regularly rehearse the failings of your family, friends, coworkers, or fellow church members? Are you more people's accuser or their advocate?

Remember that love is kind. And if it's not kind, it's not love.

4

Love Is a Battlefield

Love does not envy.

1 Corinthians 13:4

This love, free from instinct, free from all duties but those which love has freely assumed, almost wholly free from jealousy, and free without qualification from the need to be needed, is eminently spiritual. It is the sort of love one can imagine between angels. Have we here found a natural love which is Love itself?

C. S. Lewis[1]

One of my high school crushes was a girl named Maura. She was a year older than me, a real sweetheart—peaceful, kind, and an easy laugher. She had these wonderful rosy cheeks. I liked her a lot. And Maura liked me a lot . . . as a friend.

Is there anything more piercing to the heart of a lovelorn boy than the Friend Zone dagger?

Maura and I spent quite a bit of time together. We went to the same school and ate lunch together almost every day. We went to church together. Our parents were friends, so we saw each other quite a bit "after hours," so to speak. And Maura and I had a lot in common. For instance, she was also hopelessly in love with someone a year older—a boy named Trevor. He was very tall, muscular, and had great hair. He was also a clear leader in our youth group. Everybody looked up to Trevor.

I hated this guy.

He was very nice to me, I should say. We didn't interact a whole lot, but Trevor did not appear to have any negative qualities. He was every Christian young girl's dream boy. But I hated him because he was a constant reminder to me that I was *not* every Christian young girl's dream boy.

Trevor was everything I wasn't. He had everything I wanted, especially Maura's affection. The only difference was that he didn't want it. Yes, I found myself pining for a girl who didn't care because she was pining for a boy who didn't care. What a sorry lot we were.

For his part, Trevor did nothing wrong. But I watched him like a hawk, looking for some kind of deficiency. I mentally rehearsed any flaws I could find, imagining nearly all of them. I not only wanted what Trevor had, I wanted him punished for having it.

I think this kind of malicious inner thought life is what Paul has in mind in his excursus on love when he forbids envy.

You Give Love a Bad Name

Envy doesn't just constitute a failure to love our neighbor. It is first and foremost a failure to love God. Envying others is one way we say to God, "You have failed me. I am dissatisfied with you."

The original sin may be that of pride, but it quickly gives root to a flourishing of countless deadly sins, one of which gives rise to the first recorded murder in the Bible.

Envy is not mentioned explicitly in the Genesis 4 account of Cain's killing of his brother Abel, but it is there glowing radioactively between the lines.

> Now Abel became a shepherd of flocks, but Cain worked the ground. In the course of time Cain presented some of the land's produce as an offering to the LORD. And Abel also presented an offering—some of the firstborn of his flock and their fat portions. The LORD had regard for Abel and his offering, but he did not have regard for Cain and his offering. Cain was furious, and he looked despondent.

Then the LORD said to Cain, "Why are you furious? And why do you look despondent? If you do what is right, won't you be accepted? But if you do not do what is right, sin is crouching at the door. Its desire is for you, but you must rule over it."

Cain said to his brother Abel, "Let's go out to the field." And while they were in the field, Cain attacked his brother Abel and killed him. (Gen. 4:2–8)

God had accepted Abel's offering but not Cain's. Cain had put lots of effort into his offering; it was the fruit of his agricultural labors. He felt slighted by God. Abel had God's favor, and Cain did not. Cain burned against his brother. He wanted what his brother received—the Lord's approval. His envy turned to wrath, and his wrath turned to murder.

Envy has been corrupting our love ever since.

In an echo of 1 Timothy 6:10 on money being the root of all kinds of evil, James 3:16 tells us, "For where there is envy and selfish ambition, there is disorder and every evil practice." James goes on to say:

What is the source of wars and fights among you? Don't they come from your passions that wage war within you? You desire and do not have. You murder and covet and cannot obtain. You fight and wage war. You do not have because you do not ask. (4:1–2)

The use of "passions" here is rather interesting. Love, of course, is a passion. And envy is a kind of perversion of love. It's what happens when we love things more than people. It's what happens when we love only what people may do for us or give to us. Love can become envy when we only see people as rivals or a means to an end. Because the lost world does not know the centering source of Love himself, envy runs rampant within it. Consider the observation of the prophet Ezekiel when he's carried by the Spirit of God to witness the detestable acts of the pagans: his vision begins at the gate where an "offensive statue that provokes jealousy was located" (Ezek. 8:3).

Envy is a disordered worship, which is a disordered love. You cannot envy someone and love them at the same time. And once we depart the house of love to enter the street of envy, we find ourselves drifting in and out of other sins along the way. The self-worship of pride leads to the others-hatred of envy, and envy can then lead to theft, lust, adultery, bitterness, malice, and murder.

And envy is a genius of an enemy because it passes itself off as being on our side.

A World without Love

The best sermon I've ever heard on envy was preached by Matt Kruse, a pastor in the Boston area. Kruse's pivotal illustration involved recalling a time he was driving out of New York City. At a fork in the road, he took the path he thought would be most swift only to find himself sitting in bumper-to-bumper traffic. From his stationary position he fumed, watching as the traffic in the option he hadn't taken zipped along speedily.

Matt was frustrated. He grew bitter. As his impatience and anger grew, his feelings toward the faceless strangers passing by on the parallel road grew more and more in animosity.

Instead of thinking of all the wonderful things he'd experienced on his trip to New York, instead of thinking of the blessing of his family being present in the car with him, instead of thinking of all the great things that lay ahead for him, he chose to look to the side, to what others had that, at the moment, he didn't. Envy is that "sideways glance," Matt said, and it's a killer.

Envy's sideways glance is a complex snare; it mixes self-pity with covetousness, self-centeredness with desire, and bitterness with the boundlessness of our imagination.

Envy is dangerous to our souls, because it is inherently disobedient to God's specific command to love our neighbors as ourselves. First Corinthians 13:4 says, "Love does not envy." Why? Because godly love is selfless and self-sacrificial; it seeks to invest in others for their good. Envy, on the other hand, is selfish and self-indulgent; it resents others and is at odds with their good. Love can give us a taste of heaven in this world. Envy makes people not our neighbors but our rivals. Like lust, envy objectifies others, treating them like vending machines to be used, dispensers of our fulfillment and satisfaction.

Envy gives us a world without love, a kind of living hell.

Can't Buy Me Love

Jerry Bridges writes, "*Envy* is the painful and oftentimes resentful awareness of an advantage enjoyed by someone else."[2] And this "painful awareness" Bridges refers to is the irritation or angst our covetous desire prompts in us. For the most part, however, we usually don't find envy painful at all but a quite pleasurable petting of our egos.

What is envy? Envy is resentful desire for what someone else has or *is*. This means that envy is not simply about stuff; it is also about character traits, gifts, blessings, families, positions in life. I can be as equally envious of you because you own a Mercedes as I can because you make friends very easily. I want what you have, and I hate you for having it. When I'm in envy mode, relationships merely become currency, means of buying what I want without a care to whom I may be bankrupting of love.

The qualifier "resentful" is key to understanding envious desire. Titus 3:3 lumps envy in with malice, hate, and "detesting one another." James 3:14 qualifies envy as "bitter." The implications seem clear: envy involves a negative feeling toward the person who has or is what we want or want to be. In other words, envy doesn't just want what someone else has or is; it doesn't want that someone else to have or be it *either*.

Again, we see in Matthew 27:18 that the religious leaders turned in Jesus for torture and crucifixion because they envied him. They weren't just jealous of his following or his power; they didn't just covet his ministry and reputation; they wanted him dead. In this sense, as easy as it is to envy, it is also completely irrational.

J. R. Miller agrees: "Envy is a most unworthy passion. It is utterly without reason. It is pure malevolence, revealing the worst spirit. Cain was angry with Abel, because he was good."[3]

The irrational nature of envy reveals just how ridiculously idolatrous it is. Envy is one fist shaken at God in defiance and the other poised in militant self-assertion. When we are envious, we imagine ourselves as gods, rulers of *what ought to be.* We think that the will that should be done on earth is ours.

There are two key ways envy attempts to usurp divine prerogatives belonging only to God himself. These are our attempts at an envious coup d'état of the Good Shepherd.

First, envy is ultimately about self-justification. "I should have that or be that," we say, reasoning from what we imagine we deserve. We do not see ourselves as falling short of God's glory but as being denied glory we are owed. Envy is a way of denying our need to be justified before God and affirming our blasphemous belief that we need no justification, only tribute and satisfaction. That is the first way envy pridefully presumes God's place.

Second, envy is also about self-sovereignty, about the need for control over what is right and wrong, just and unjust. When we are envious, we are making determinations about what people should or shouldn't have. Cain hated Abel both because Abel's offering was accepted and because his own was not. By unleashing the wrath that only belongs to God, in a perversion of justice, Cain asserts his own sovereignty. Envy denies that "the LORD gives, and the LORD takes away" (Job 1:21), saying, "No—*I* do."

Envy is willful forgetfulness of God. With that in mind, consider Proverbs 23:17: "Don't let your heart envy sinners; instead, always fear the LORD."

As we can see, envy is fundamentally blasphemous and therefore fundamentally dangerous, not least because we find ourselves slipping into it quite easily. We are masters of self-justification. So many times we don't feel bad about envying someone; in fact, we hardly notice we envy them at all.

Love Has No Pride

My friend Steve Bezner tells a story of being college room-mates with a budding evangelical superstar.

> There are three small-ish Christian universities in Abilene. During our student years, a weekly college Bible study met where students from all over the city would gather on Thursday nights for prayer, worship, and a time of teaching. The study was growing, and there was word that the pastor . . . was looking to hand off leadership.
>
> I hoped they would choose me. I was, after all, a great student and a decent communicator.
>
> Instead, they chose Matt.
>
> And that's when the jealousy began.
>
> The weekly Bible study swelled in attendance to approximately 2,000 students—in Abilene! Matt was receiving invitations to speak all over West Texas. In one story that became an almost-legend among our apartment, a man sold him a car for the incredible price of one dollar. He was becoming the local spiritual authority, and he was in his early twenties.
>
> I was amazed at God's blessing on Matt's life.
>
> And I badly wanted it for myself.
>
> I don't know if you've ever been jealous of someone you were simultaneously friends with. It is a difficult spiritual condition to describe. On the one hand, I was happy for my friend. He was experiencing the sort of ministry success that is impossible to orchestrate. God was clearly ordaining a path for him. On the other hand, I felt slighted. I felt I had worked harder; I felt I had "paid my dues." Why was he getting to live the life I wanted to live?

To add insult to injury, I was now known around campus and around town by a new label: "Matt Chandler's Roommate."[4]

I, too, have friends I am tempted to envy. I am ashamed at how easily I can succumb to this sin. When I was pastoring, I was sometimes given to envy when another church in my area was growing more quickly than mine. Or it could be as simple as seeing another pastor receiving positive comments on his Sunday sermon from his own congregants on Facebook while mine hardly seemed interested in my sermon. It happens to me today whenever an author friend or peer achieves some publishing milestone that eludes me. If his or her new book appears to sell better than mine. If his or her book gets better notices on higher profile websites or magazines. If his or her book wins an award? Forget about it. I can feel the burn just thinking about it.

I also know I struggle with envy because of my enjoyment when it is somehow satisfied. Remember, envy isn't just wanting what someone has—it's wanting them *not* to have it. I rarely feel this way about friends, but I certainly feel this way from time to time about imaginary nemeses or people I just plain don't like. When someone I don't like suffers a setback, when I know their book hasn't sold very well, when I see them getting snubbed or they're just otherwise discouraged or embarrassed, my hellish nature rears up with delight. The German term for this is *schadenfreude* (pronounced "shodden-froida"). It is pleasure taken at another's misfortune.

Schadenfreude is what *America's Funniest Home Videos* is based upon! But in my world, it has less to do with finding glee in someone getting nailed in the privates by an errant baseball or by slipping off a diving board and more to do with secretly reveling in another's embarrassment. Social media these days tends to run on *schadenfreude*. We love watching the people we hate fail. And how do we know we hate them? We love to see them fail.

This, too, is a kind of envy. And we have to root it out of us if we want to be lovers, not haters. We have to take a ruthless self-inventory if we want to manifest the love of Christ in our lives.

Because envy is sly and self-justifying, it is important that we self-reflect and ask ourselves penetrating questions to identify its presence in our hearts. Envy can look and feel like many different things; it is an excellent chameleon. Sometimes envy of those who have money can masquerade as crusading for those who don't. Sometimes envy of someone's gifts can disguise itself as helping the ungifted. There are lots of otherwise good things that can become tainted when done out of envy. Many people get good at passive-aggressive behavior because of the subtle hold envy has on their hearts.

Below are some questions to ask yourself in diagnosing envy's presence in your life. Consider them seriously and be as honest with yourself as you can.

1. Have you ever been confronted about treating a certain group of people (rich, educated, good-looking, popular, talented, etc.) poorly?
2. Whether it's been noticed by others or not, do you find yourself having negative feelings toward a certain person or group of people without personal cause?

3. Do you find yourself despising or otherwise looking down on celebrities or people with high-profile platforms?

4. Are you prone to judging people according to their appearances?

5. Do you sometimes feel threatened by people with similar looks, gifts, jobs, or callings as you?

6. As a woman or man, do you often "size up" other women or men in the room, measuring how they compare with you according to appearance, stature, attention, or influence?

7. Is it difficult for you to enjoy the successes of others? Do you resent others' successes, whether friends or not?

8. Do you tend to "stew" on the idea that some people have blessings you don't think they deserve?

9. Do you engage in *schadenfreude*?

10. Are you nagged by a constant feeling of discontentment?

11. Do you struggle with "sideways glances"?

Answering yes to one or two of these questions doesn't necessarily mean you have a problem with envy, but it is certainly cause for closer inspection of your heart. Ask God to help you see if the roots of envy are present there, hidden where you can't see them. If you answered yes to more than a few of these questions, there's no doubt about it: envy has you in its grip.

It's time to get a crushing grip on envy.

Conducting a ruthless self-inventory like the one that begins with the questions above is the first step to attacking the pride at the root of our envy. It is our way of saying to God and to ourselves, "I want my love to be real."

Would You Fight for My Love?

Loving others the way we have been loved by God is a daily work of death. It requires all the vigor and violence of taking up our cross and following Jesus. But with the power of grace, we can do it. Here's how.

First, it may be necessary just to get some perspective. Pull yourself out of the tall grass of your own interior world. Reevaluate the value of temporary things versus the eternal. It's a familiar story line in the familiar crime stats: a young man murders another young man because he wants his expensive sneakers. The irrationality of envy has taken over. In envy's perverted economy, tennis shoes are worth more than human life. If you'll pardon the understatement, this perspective is clearly out of whack.

Before we congratulate ourselves for being above such heinous crimes, we need to realize that our sense of perspective is just as prone to envy's perversion. We engage in a wish-fulfillment fantasy similar to the kid who thinks somebody else's shoes are the solution to his happiness whenever we play what Stephen Altrogge calls the "if only" game.

Here's how the "if only" game works. Think about what would make you happy. I mean really, freakishly, "I can't believe this is happening to me" happy. What do you obsess about, dream about, desperately hope for?

Now put the words "if only" in front of that dream. *If only I could get married, then I would be really happy. If only I could get the job promotion that would get me out of cubicle-land and into the corner office, then I would be satisfied. If only my wife weren't sick so often . . . if only my son would start respecting me . . . if only my budget wasn't so tight, then I'd have peace, joy, contentment, and some sleep at night. . . .*

Most people are good at playing the "if only" game. The only problem is, you can never win.[5]

Envy is the result of upside-down values, so just like the kid who shoots another kid for his shoes won't be satisfied just with those shoes but will want to continue his sinful ways to accumulate more, we, too, won't be satisfied when we get what we wish for. We will then wish for something else. When we play the "if only" game, we will always be stuck with the last-place medal called envy. But if we adjust our sideways glance to a different kind of comparison, we suddenly don't feel like such losers.

Have you noticed how when we look to the side to compare ourselves, we always look at people who have more than we do? Why don't we compare ourselves with people who have less than we do, who are worse off than we are?

In 2011, Hurricane Irene stormed across the Northeast coast. Irene did not do as much damage as predicted but it did devastate parts of Vermont and Connecticut and other portions of New York and New England. I remember having a conversation with a woman whose Brooklyn apartment was flooded with waist-high water, the third such flooding she'd endured in a one-month span. She said, "After having to clean up thoroughly and have professionals guard against mold for the third time, I was feeling very sorry for myself. Then I looked up footage of Hurricane Katrina on YouTube."

Instead of reflecting on what she didn't have that others did, she decided to reflect on what she had that others didn't. Sure, her apartment was flooded, but she didn't lose everything. She was alive and safe. Insurance covered replacements and repairs. All things considered, she had a lot of reasons to be thankful, not mournful.

This is the kind of sideways glance that would benefit most of us. Whenever we're tempted to anxiety or irritation about the quality of our job, house, car, electronic goods, or what-have-you, we ought to ponder the plight of the urban poor or those in developing countries who don't know when they'll get their next meal. When we compare ourselves to people truly struggling to survive, we stifle envy.

But this kind of perspective only goes so far. There is yet a more enduring counter to envy, and it's remembering in every circumstance and situation that we have too much to be grateful for to grumble.

When God's love is always available to us, we have ongoing grounds for thanksgiving. Discontentment comes from a feeling of being owed. Envy is the enemy of contentment because it is always focused on what we don't have. But if we train ourselves to be thankful, envy's muscle will entropy.

It will not feel natural to "give thanks in everything" (1 Thess. 5:18) at first, but the more we are intentional about doing it, the more natural it will become. You may need to write little notes to yourself as reminders or tie a string around your wrist. Listen to a different kind of music on your morning commute. Begin the habit of giving thanks before every meal, snack, and cup of coffee. Incorporate whatever little practices or reminders you think will help you remember to offer thanks to God for who he is and what he's done.

When we intentionally switch our mode to thankfulness, we see all that God gives us is sufficient because *he* is sufficient. And if he were to take things away from us—our possessions, our job, our health—we would be in a better position to praise him anyway. When Christ alone is our treasure, thankfulness for his "incalculable riches" (Eph. 3:8) gives envy no purchase in our souls.

It is not for nothing that Proverbs 14:30 tells us, "A tranquil heart is life to the body, but jealousy is rottenness to the bones."

Finally, consider these words from 1 Peter 2:1–3:

> Therefore, rid yourselves of all malice, all deceit, hypocrisy, envy, and all slander. Like newborn infants, desire the pure milk of the word, so that by it you may grow up into your salvation, if you have tasted that the Lord is good.

If you find the Lord good, your longing for stuff wanes. And you will long more for the pure spiritual milk when you have tasted and seen that the gospel is satisfying. And that is really the biggest battle to fight in your own heart and mind to conquer envy: believing the gospel.

The antidote for the self-justification and the self-sovereignty driving envy is rootedness in justification by faith and the supremacy of Christ. Like all other sins, envy is fundamentally a sin of pride, and the only way to kill pride is to confess our sin, repent of it, and believe in the forgiveness given to us by God's free grace in Jesus.

Flashing back to Genesis 4, why do you think Abel's sacrifice was accepted and Cain's was not? Did God just like Abel better? Did Abel know the right religious words or jump through the right religious hoops?

No, Abel's sacrifice was accepted first because it was the sort of offering God had commanded and also because his offering of sacrificed livestock best reflected the stakes of making us right with God. After the fall, one of the first things Adam and Eve did to cover their shame was clothe themselves with plants. But they had brought death into the world and bloodshed; only bloodshed could cover their shame. So God replaced their leafy garments with animal skins. This is how serious sin is; this is how serious envy is. Something has to die. "Without the shedding of blood there is no forgiveness" (Heb. 9:22).

God required an offering, and Abel brought real sacrifices. Cain brought the fruit of his hard work. We cannot and will not satisfy the debt of envy through the fruit of our hard work any more than Cain could. If we want to kill envy, it will take death.

Thanks be to God, then, that Jesus offers himself as the acceptable sacrifice. The fruit of his hard work culminates with his substitutionary death: taking our place, covering our shame, killing our sin.

In one of the great glorious ironies of the gospel, it is envy for what Jesus has that drives us to betray him and nail him to the cross, but in his crucifixion he is gladly, willingly, humbly, and freely giving us everything he's got. No one is more generous than our Lord. We need not envy him or anyone else; his unclenched hand freely gives us all things! So says Paul: "He did not even spare his own Son but gave him up for us all. How will he not also with him grant us everything?" (Rom. 8:32).

So, then, envy is not only spiritual suicide, it is spiritual nonsense! Not one of us can add an ounce of satisfaction through a pound of envy. But in the free gift of eternal life there is eternal fulfillment.

The final and best way to assassinate envy, therefore, is to park ourselves at the foot of the cross early and often. Rather than constantly fooling with envy's sideways glance, we ought to be "keeping our eyes on Jesus, the pioneer and perfecter of our faith" (Heb. 12:2). Look at him and his glory, and you will find rest.

If you want to kill envy and become a better lover of others, by love, make war on your flesh.

5

No Ordinary Love

Love . . . is not boastful, is not arrogant, is not rude, is not self-seeking, is not irritable.

1 Corinthians 13:4–5

I will honestly admit that many, many times in my life I have been startled in wonder over the fact that love thereby at times seemed to lose everything, even though it gains everything.

Søren Kierkegaard[1]

I am so stunningly not like Jesus.

I feel this reality most deeply whenever I interact with another person, which of course is when my being like Jesus matters most!

It usually happens like this: I come home from work, which aside from teaching a couple of classes and conducting a few casual conversations, I have largely spent in my own mental world. I spend a lot of time by myself. And it's draining. So when I get home, I want to be by myself. But home is where the people live who matter the most to me. And they get my leftover interest, my leftover energy, my leftover love.

Tired and self-pitying, I then see every request, no matter how small, as the straw that broke the camel's back. Every request for my help or interest becomes a bridge too far. After I pull into my driveway, I shift my self-interest into drive as I put my car into park.

This happens throughout my day as well, as texts and emails and phone calls pile up, little intrusions piercing my force field of self-worship. Every interruption is a usurping of my being the center of the universe. It happened even as I was composing this chapter. I was at my seminary office writing when I received a text message from my wife about a couple of household issues we're currently dealing with. Our hot water's been out for six days now, and a freezer we keep in the garage apparently shut off and everything in it spoiled before we noticed the smell of death wafting into the house. She was asking about a plan for cleaning out the garage. I was immediately irritated. Didn't she know I was writing?

Well, no, she didn't know what I was doing, because I wasn't at home. And on top of that, there was no note on the message marking it "Urgent" or saying "You must respond immediately." That's just how I read it, because I was busy and didn't want to be bothered. Because I'd rather wrongly attribute selfishness to others than rightly to myself.

And then I think of Jesus with all the pressing needs and interruptions in the course of his business. I think of him stopping to heal a frightened woman with a bleeding issue while on the way to help a man whose daughter was about to die (and who did die while Jesus stopped to talk to the woman). Jesus didn't get bothered by the interruptions in his ministry. He actually saw the interruptions *as* his ministry.

Jesus was perfect, and yet he did not look down on others. I am ridiculously imperfect, but I do look down on others. Jesus was perfectly holy, and yet was not arrogant. I am frustratingly unholy, but I am arrogant a lot. Like, *a lot*.

I am not Jesus. But I do want to be like him.

Jesus had so many opportunities to go around like a puffed-up narcissist, and as he was God incarnate, you might think he should have. But even as he was saying things like "I am the way, the truth, and the life" (John 14:6) and basically preaching himself as the true center of the universe, we never get the impression he was pridefully boasting. He was humble. He was lowly. He was gentle.

As the very embodiment of love, Jesus cannot be what love is not. But I can.

Paul says that love "is not boastful, is not arrogant, is not rude, is not self-seeking, is not irritable" (1 Cor. 13:4–5). Even in my solitude, even in my quiet, my self-centeredness is a spiritual boasting in myself. It's this kind of boasting in myself that leads to my arrogance, which then prompts my rudeness and reinforces my self-seeking through irritability.

True love is essentially a decentering of self.

Deep down in the recesses of every human soul is a cloying, ravenous monster ruthless for its own glory. This monster clambers out of its dark pit constantly, hunting and gathering food and trinkets—even collecting feelings and experiences—especially hungry for adulation and affirmation. It is never satisfied with these things, so its stomach is always grumbling for more. This monster is *us*. Rather, it is the sinful nature in us. Paul describes how this monster competes with his other inner desire—to love and obey God—this way:

> For in my inner self I delight in God's law, but I see a different law in the parts of my body, waging war against the law of my mind and taking me prisoner to the law of sin in the parts of my body. What a wretched man I am! Who will rescue me from this body of death? (Rom. 7:22–24)

"This body of death" is at constant war with our freedom in Christ. This is why Jesus says we must crucify the monster every day. "If anyone wants to follow after me, let him deny himself, take up his cross daily, and follow me" (Luke 9:23).

The monster to be killed inside of us is pride.

Every one of us harbors pride in our deepest-seated self, so appeasement of pride is the chief industry of all humankind.

From the things we buy to the relationships we participate in to even our motivations for things like work or family or leisure, when we are losing the battle of self-denial, feeding the pride monster is our greatest passion. The pride-appeasement industry is booming, because demand is always high, and therefore so is supply.

On the magazine racks at the grocery store we now find titles like *All You* and *Self*, no longer bothering to veil attempts at the subject we are most interested in. (I sometimes joke with a friend who subscribes to these titles that we should start a magazine called *Others*. But we know it wouldn't sell!) Because we are all by default conspicuous consumers, consumer culture is predicated on our inalienable belief that we are the sun around which everything orbits. The cable company Comcast now even has an ad campaign where actress Jane Lynch assures customers of that very thing, saying directly, "You are the center of the universe."

This is all blasphemy. The Christian message begins with the stark realization that we are not the center of the universe. Like the character Leo in *Titanic*, we stand at the bow of the ship, spreading our arms to span the horizon, not realizing we're headed for disaster. We proclaim, "I'm the king of the world!"

Then the ship sinks.

Pride (in the Name of Love)

In *The Silmarillion*, the "prequel" of sorts to the classic trilogy The Lord of the Rings, author J. R. R. Tolkien crafts a parallel to the creation and fall of Satan. Eru is the great creator of Middle Earth, but before time began, he created the Ainur, a legion of spirits (angels) to reflect his own thoughts. Eru taught the Ainur to play a great musical composition. Together the music they played was powerful and majestic, and it reflected Eru's glory. But one of the Ainur named Melkor, whom Eru had especially gifted with knowledge and power, departed from the symphony to create his own song. The result was dissonance.

With this story, Tolkien illustrates for us how pride is fundamentally a rebellion against God's plan and the indulging of our desire to, in effect, "toot our own horn." Tolkien is playing off the traditional account of the fall of Satan, of course, but he has provided a powerful image of the way fallen humanity attempts to steal God's glory.

God created all of us with the capacity to worship. We are never *not* worshiping. Before the fall, Adam and Eve worshiped God only. But when they willfully succumbed to the serpent's temptation to "be like God" (Gen. 3:5), the wires of worship got crossed. They placed themselves on the thrones of their hearts. And ever since, all while God's Word and his creation are declaring his glory, we're departing from the song to sing of our own.

The pride monster devours everything in its path, seeking its own satisfaction, its own centrality, and therefore its own glory. We see this in everything from the nagging desire to "keep up with the Joneses" to the propensity to become a "me-monster" in social situations. It comes out even in passive aggression and manipulative silence. You don't have to be loudly and obnoxiously bragging to be prideful; you can be withholding affection or service. Sometimes pride looks like sullen retreat, selfish solitude, or quiet judgmentalism.

Sometimes we toot our own horn in the privacy of our own thoughts.

Boastfulness, arrogance, rudeness, irritability. What are these but symptoms of self-centrality, of pride?

I struggle with this not just with people who love me but with people who hate me. Some internet troll or "discernment blogger" puts me in their crosshairs and fires away. They've got a list of reasons why I'm a terrible person. And I think, *You don't even know me. If you did, you'd see that I'm actually quite impressive.*

But inside I know that's not true. In fact, I'm often worse than they think I am. They don't know the half of it! If they could actually see inside of me, they'd see me for who I really am. I may not be an awful person the way they think I am, but all my efforts to disguise my rottenness can't get rid of it. In his classic devotional work, *A Serious Call to a Devout and Holy Life*, William Law puts it this way:

> Let a man but consider that if the world knew all of him that he knows of himself—if they saw what vanity and passions govern him inside and what secret tempers sully and corrupt his best actions—he would have no more pretense to be honored and admired for his goodness and wisdom than a rotten and distempered body to be loved and admired for its beauty and comeliness.[2]

Ohh-kay.

Look, we're all frauds of one kind or another. Even when we try to humble ourselves, our motives are mixed. Sin taints everything we do. Even our self-deprecation is an appeal for pity.

In many relationships, this is often how pride manifests: playing the part of the loser, the sad sack, the pitiful one, the martyr. We are passive-aggressive, leeching off the emotionality of others to prop ourselves up and feel better about ourselves. We use our hurt feelings or our need for love to manipulate others, to guilt-trip them. This is just as self-seeking as bombastic arrogance or hostile demands.

D. A. Carson says, "Lovelessness breeds thousands of variations on inferiority complexes and superiority complexes."[3] We are endlessly innovative when it comes to the way pride works out in our relationships. If being condescending or snippy with you won't work, I'll play the victim. I'll get overly defensive and turn the tables. I'll make you apologize for something I did.

Do you know people like that?

Are *you* a person like that?

Is it any wonder, then, that Jesus said that in order to follow him, we have to crucify ourselves?

This Is the Way Love Is

Here's one of the shifts I have to make in order to put a nail in my flesh: when the text messages come in that interrupt "my day," I stop and remember that the person on the other end has a day of their own. Like mine, it could be going well or badly. Like me, they have concerns, needs, and worries. Like me, they are made in the image of God. And my response to them—or lack of response to them—can help them either feel that reality or have it stifled.

I try to advocate in my heart and mind for the source of the interruption. If it's my wife, I remind myself that she works hard to make our home a great place to be for our family and for those we love. I assign good motives to her, not careless ones. If she's texting me midmorning to ask about the stench coming from the broken freezer, it's not because she's thinking, *How can I ruin Jared's day?* She's thinking, *We have people coming over soon, and I'm not sure exactly what to do. Maybe Jared can help.* She has ascribed intelligence and helpfulness to me! And here I am frustrated by it.

I think of when I was pastoring and how often I suffered from my congregation's careless words, backhanded compliments, or even silent neglect. The temptation was always to stew about it, to get resentful or bitter, to hold it against them. Instead, though, I would try to imagine sympathetic circumstances that could give rise to such things. Maybe they were dealing with a very difficult time at home or work, and their emotional reservoir was just tapped out. That didn't make it okay to treat me (or anyone else) poorly, but it helped me not think too poorly of them in return.

Maybe they just never learned to communicate well. A lot of people grow up in homes where conflict is handled by one of two extremes—loudness or silence. They either learned how to resolve problems by yelling or never learned to resolve them at all. Without conscious and concentrated effort to change, everybody's communication style is simply the product of their upbringing.

Or maybe that person responded poorly to me because they misunderstood me. Or maybe they were just tired. There could be a thousand reasons that don't excuse sin but nevertheless help us advocate for others in our hearts.

And one big reason we ought to think this way about others is because this is exactly what we would want them to do for us. This is Golden Rule love (Matt. 7:12). Do you want every careless word or mistake you've made to be held against you in perpetuity? Do you really want people to treat you according to your worst moments? Do you hope people assume the worst about you? Or do you want them to forgive you? To bear all things, believe all things, hope all things, endure all things (1 Cor. 13:7)?

The command from God is straightforward: "Do not take revenge or bear a grudge against members of your community, but love your neighbor as yourself" (Lev. 19:18). Jesus, of course, later reiterates this imperative as the second part of what we call the Great Commandment:

> Love the Lord your God with all your heart, with all your soul, with all your mind, and with all your strength. The second is, Love your neighbor as yourself. There is no other command greater than these. (Mark 12:30–31)

What he's done is make our love for God and our love for others inextricable from each other. Not because others are on the same level as God, of course, but because our failure to love others is essentially an issue of self-worship. It is idolatry. We are making ourselves higher than God. So when we center on God, loving him with everything, we have logically decentered ourselves, which frees us to love others affectionately and sacrificially.

The beauty of this dynamic is found in the person and work of Christ himself. Jesus did not regard equality with God as something to be exploited but rather emptied himself (Phil. 2:6–7), not of his deity, of course, but of his right to self-protection. He put the will of the Father ahead of his own (Luke 22:42), selflessly accepting the need for sacrifice, and thereby demonstrating the perfect love of God and at the same time perfect love for sinners.

Jesus shows us the way of *agape* love, a love that is oriented toward others sacrificially for their good and glory. Embracing this way of love puts us in the position of emptying ourselves, of dying to ourselves. Loving others this way makes Jesus look very big.

But how do we get there?

Most of us are prepared to love others only up to the point where it begins to actually cost us. We operate in the spirit of the Meat Loaf song: "I would do anything for love. But I won't do that." How do we move from self-interested love to self-sacrificial love?

Well, I know I am less prone to *agape* love when I've taken my eyes off Jesus. The more time I spend with him in the Bible and in prayer, the more "on my mind" he becomes outside of those times. And spending time gazing at Jesus in his Word actually has the supernatural effect, by the power of the Holy Spirit, to make me more like him (2 Cor. 3:18).

The problem is that you and I spend far too much time thinking about ourselves and far too little thinking about Jesus.

Fixing our eyes on Christ (Heb. 12:2) cultivates in us a kind of self-forgetfulness. Our fixation on ourselves can be so deceptive. Even to get bogged down in how we're not like Jesus doesn't put us in the position to become more like Jesus! Dwelling in our inadequacy or imperfection only breeds self-pity or despair. So even an inordinate focus on "how I'm doing" won't cut it.

This is the crucial difference between being self-aware and being self-*conscious*.

The self-conscious person has trouble loving others because he's constantly thinking of himself. He's worried what others think of him or how he's coming across. He's not just aware of his deficiencies; he's mired in them. The self-aware person, on the other hand, is better able to love others because she knows her weaknesses and besetting sins, which include an obsessive preoccupation with herself!

The self-conscious person only sees his obstacles to love. The self-aware person isn't overcome by the obstacles; she knows they're there and strategizes to overcome them.

This isn't a trick. It may sound like splitting hairs, but it really is the difference between staring at ourselves and looking to Jesus. We have to really *behold* him, and in the light of his glory we certainly see our sins and frailties, but we also see his joy and his power—exactly what we need to become less fixated on ourselves and more oriented toward others.

The love of Jesus is the alternate reality to a fallen world operating according to fleshly desires and appetites. It is the real reality, the heavenly state of things, of which this world, even with its loves and joys, is but a pale reflection.

Love is the operating system of the kingdom of God. But because Jesus is building his kingdom, and because the Spirit of God indwells the soul of every true follower of Jesus, we have the opportunity every day to bring a little taste of heaven into the world wherever we go.

In Romans 12:10, Paul envisions this deeper and realer reality showing itself like this: "Love one another deeply as brothers and sisters. Take the lead in honoring one another."

In the English Standard Version, that latter part is translated to read, "Outdo one another in showing honor."

This is the way of true love: working hard to out-love each other!

Imagine what our relationships would be like if we were all trying to outdo one another this way. We don't even have to wait for the other to participate. We can start right now. We can make it our goal to outdo others in forgiveness, mercy, generosity, and comfort. If we're willing to die to ourselves. To outdo one another, we have to be willing to out-die one another.

Anything less is a kind of living a lie. Dallas Willard writes, "[Christ's] death was a revelation of the nature of basic reality. Without knowledge of it and its meaning, we are desperately ignorant of reality, and therefore all our thinking can only result in monstrous falsehoods."[4]

And because the death (and resurrection) of Jesus is the most significant event in history, proving once for all that our deepest desire—to be totally known and at the same time totally loved—can be satisfied by God himself, when we love others sacrificially, we become a living apologetic for this reality. The gospel doesn't need us. It isn't empowered by us or dependent upon us in any way. But by our love, we can make the gospel ring true to others.

"This is how we have come to know love: He laid down his life for us. We should also lay down our lives for our brothers and sisters" (1 John 3:16). There is no greater love than this (John 15:13). Jesus's death proves God's disposition toward sinners. And ours does too.

And when we commit to self-sacrificing love, the way of Christ becomes more and more evident in our life and the lives around us. Jesus even promises us that if we will love this way, we will discover a greater joy, a greater life than we could even imagine. So much of our lovelessness is a manifestation of self-protection, of self-exaltation, but the end result is self-abasement and self-degradation. Jesus says if you want to find your life, you will be willing to lose it (Matt. 16:25). You will find a flourishing resurrection kind of life on the other side of the grave you put your pride in. Francis Schaeffer writes:

> The Bible is not speaking of some romantic feeling, some idealization, some abstraction. Jesus carries this concept of facing the rejection, being slain, down into a very practical situation: facing an alien world. It is the saying "no" to self when our natural selves would desire acceptance by the alien world—a world in revolt against its Creator and our Lord. As we look at the New Testament as a whole, we find that this command of Christ is not limited to one situation, it is that which is to be the whole mentality and outlook of the Christian's life. What is being presented to us here is the question of the Christian's mentality in all of life, and the order stands: rejected, slain, raised. As Christ's rejection and death are the first steps in the order of redemption, so our rejection and death to things and self are the first steps in the order of true and growing spirituality.[5]

This is why Paul resolved only to know Christ crucified (1 Cor. 2:2). He knew he couldn't keep his own life anyway. Better to find it eternally in Christ through dying with him.

The life that Christ gives to all who will die in him and to themselves is eternal life. This doesn't just mean it goes on forever after you die. That's true! But it also means that you have this real life living inside of you right this very moment. And all the moments that threaten to dislodge your hope or steal your joy or just plain ol' rub you the wrong way. Eternal life helps us "take up our cross daily," to die to our self through our coworker getting the promotion we were passed over for, through our neighbor letting their dog poop in our yard (again), through all the antisocial habits of the irritating people standing in line around us at the airport or in the grocery store. Eternal life helps us die to our self when our spouse has "forgotten" to put dirty clothes in the hamper (again) or dirty dishes in the sink (again). When we are confronted with bad breath, skid marks in the underwear, the sound of chewing, snoring, the cold shoulder at bedtime, a million little annoyances and irritations that pile up and threaten our sense of self-centeredness, we remember the cross of Christ where all the things wrong about us were crucified with him. He comes near to us in love. On what basis do we deny others the same?

We are faced every day with so many opportunities to remember we are not the center of the universe, that God has commanded us to love others as we love ourselves, knowing that when it came right down to it, the One who is the center of the universe was willing to do it first.

Love in Hard Times

Once upon a time, as Jesus was about to begin a trip, he was interrupted by a very important man who wanted to know what he had to do to be saved. "Good teacher," the man said, "what must I do to inherit eternal life?" (Mark 10:17).

The ensuing exchange is very brief, but it is incredibly revealing. First, we notice that the man appears to think there is something he can do to earn salvation. We later learn he is a rich man—indeed, this passage is often titled "The Rich Young Ruler"—and so he is probably used to thinking about everything in terms of currency. Now he wants to know, essentially, "What will eternal life cost me?"

Second, we notice that he is sure he is as wealthy in righteousness as he is in material possessions. Jesus reminds him of some of the key commandments to holiness: don't murder, don't commit adultery, don't steal, don't lie, and so on. The man proudly says, "I'm good with all of that. I've got a perfect record since childhood!"

But because Jesus is God, he knows everything this guy has done. He also knows exactly what this guy *is doing*. The rich young ruler is trying to pay his way into the kingdom with his morality. But Jesus knows he is not as moral as he thinks he is. And he proves it by touching the one area of his life he has not surrendered to the centrality of God. Jesus tells the man to go sell everything he has and give the money to the poor (Mark 10:21).

Jesus puts his finger on the young man's real object of worship. And what happens? "He was dismayed by this demand, and he went away grieving" (v. 22).

Earlier in the exchange, though, the guy had given his idolatry away, but most readers of the passage tend to miss it. It is found in the beginning, when Jesus first responds to the man's particular choice of words. Remember, he calls Jesus "Good Teacher," to which Jesus replies, "Why do you call me good? . . . No one is good except God alone" (v. 18).

Jesus wants this guy to think about the implications of what he's saying. "If only God is good, and you call me 'good,' what does that say about me?" Do the math.

Will the rich young ruler acknowledge then that Jesus is in fact God? No. He wants a religious expert to excuse his idolatry, not a Savior to crucify it. Notice that the next time the man addresses Jesus, he simply calls him "Teacher" (v. 20). He drops the modifier "good"!

The man was unwilling to center his life on Jesus, unable to die to his self-righteousness and self-centrality. He still wanted to cling to the outrageous absurdities of our works being good enough to merit God's kingdom and a love for money being compatible with a love for God.

But none of this is the most startling thing about the passage. The most amazing thing about the whole exchange—to me, anyway—is the beginning of Mark 10:21: "Looking at him, Jesus loved him."

Can you believe that? This self-righteous idol-worshiper. This guy unwilling to call Jesus God. This guy who arrogantly thought he could buy his way into the kingdom. Jesus loved him.

This means there is hope for us.

Every day we are messing up this whole thing. We make Jesus's love look puny toward others with our own fickle affections, our own self-interested attitudes, our own neglectful and graceless behavior. We go after countless worthless idols. But Jesus, looking at us, *loves us*. We sin, and Jesus loves us anyway.

Through the hardness of our hearts, despite the hardness of our circumstances, his love is intense and constant. This is the whole point of Christianity! God loves sinners. Christ died for sinners. By grace, sinners can be saved.

The key, then, to knowing true love and giving true love is being aware of God's gracious posture toward even the worst of us. No matter how bad your day's been, how screwed up you managed to prove yourself to be, how short with others and short-shrifting you are toward God himself, his love never relents. His *hesedh* is everlasting. His way toward us changes our way toward others. Richard Lovelace says, "The apprehension of God's presence is the ultimate core of genuine Christian experience, and the touchstone of its authenticity is the believer's vision of the character of God."[6]

How do you apprehend his presence with you?

Jesus isn't boastful. He's not rude. He's not arrogant. He's not self-seeking. Jesus isn't irritable.

Picture yourself returning home from a long day of work or school or running errands. You pull back into your driveway or parking lot, and you are suddenly awash with all the obligations and pressures waiting for you there. You are anticipating the little irritations. Maybe it's a spouse, children, a roommate, a parent. You have come to expect "one more thing" every time you reenter that space.

So, with a big sigh, you turn off the ignition and walk to the front door, steeling yourself against what may come next. You go in. Your heart sinks. You walk into your living room, all ready to endure someone else's thoughtlessness or to throw a little pity party for yourself, but you are startled to see someone you didn't expect waiting for you. It's Jesus. And he's sitting in *your* chair. And he says, "Come on in. Take a seat." Like he owns the place.

Reluctantly, you obey.

And Jesus says, "All right. Tell me about it."

You sigh again. Will it matter? You finally say, "I don't know where to begin."

Jesus says, "I've got all the time in the world."

And you spill your guts. Every single fear. Every single hurt. Every single wound and worry. Every single sin, even. And it all spills out of you and just seems to pile up invisibly on the floor, and when you think you've got it all out—every last weighty concern—and you feel completely out of words, you finally sputter out, "I just feel completely overwhelmed and I don't know what to do."

And Jesus looks at you with the warmest gaze you have ever seen, and he says, "Well, *yeah.*"

You have run smack into the greatest privilege any of us could ever enjoy, which is this: that we come to the end of ourselves and find there the sufficiency of Christ.

It is at the end of our rope that we find Christ is more than enough. And I have come to believe that for a great many of us—if not all of us—Christ will not become our only hope until Christ has become our only hope!

Until we've run dry and out of options and out of crutches and out of props. Until we're leaning, tottering, bent low, and beat down. When we're in the ditch, and our body is screaming but our soul is quiet in the foreboding aftermath of a great personal cataclysm, there is Christ, mighty to save. No one is our rock but he. No one is our stronghold but he. He is our only hope.

Love has a face that can be seen.

Love has a voice that can be heard.

Love has arms that hug and hands that hold.

We may not be able to see, hear, and feel them now, but someday we will. And even now he is closer than we think.

Love is real and incarnate and resurrected and glorified and reigning at the right hand of the Father. And love always lives to intercede for you.

Do you know this? I mean, more than academically?

Look, when you're alone and despondent, sitting at that dining room table in the wee hours of the night, head in your hands, wondering how you will make it through, over-burdened and overwhelmed, feeling lost and rejected and ashamed and anxious and *unloved*, and Jesus Christ walks through that door to stand under the kitchen light with you—what kind of look do you think is on his face?

This makes all the difference in the world.

What do you see in his face?

See the love of the one whose face was battered for you, one who, even while your sin was murdering him, spoke forgiveness to you. He was willing to lose his life to gain even *you*.

If that's not love, love doesn't exist.

6

True Love Tends to Forget

[Love] does not keep a record of wrongs.

1 Corinthians 13:5

For nothing, nothing at all, is more important than being assured of the forgiveness of God.

D. A. Carson[1]

Have you ever been in the argument time machine? Like, you're arguing with someone about one thing that just happened but end up in another time, another place?

"If I've told you once, I've told you a thousand times, please put your dishes in the sink. Don't just leave them lying around."

"Okay, okay—I hear you."

"Well, you say you hear me, but you obviously aren't listening. You *never listen* or you wouldn't have done it. You're so thoughtless and inconsiderate. You never listen to what I tell you. Just like when I told you not to take on that roofing job, because you weren't going to get paid on time."

Wait, what? I thought we were talking about the dishes. And now we're on the roof.

Do you see what happened? You were in the argument time machine. It started out about one thing, and it grew. Because it's not really about the dishes, it's about not listening or not being considerate. And once it's about those things, it becomes about *all the things.*

You think you're in the kitchen talking about dirty dishes but you find yourself on the roof two months ago, or wherever it is that has been stored up in the accuser just for this moment, so that you can be whisked away to defend yourself there as well. The argument time machine.

Now, of course, love would mean listening and being considerate and putting the dishes in the sink. But love would also mean not turning a momentary irritation into a catalog of sins recorded and saved up. Love doesn't do that. Love doesn't keep a record like that, and love certainly doesn't bring the record out to win arguments or make the case. Love stays out of the argument time machine. Paul says about love that it "does not keep a record of wrongs" (1 Cor. 13:5).

If you are serious about Christ being magnified in your life—if you're serious about real, gospel-rich love—you must be more interested in loving than in winning. This might mean looking for things to praise in this sinner you're in a relationship with rather than things to criticize or condemn. Or maybe it means remembering that none of us measure up to God's holy standard, yet he does not hold that against us. He rejoices over us. He treasures us, because of his great love. The way we regard each other can either magnify ourselves in self-righteousness or it can magnify Christ in our giving grace, forgiveness, and encouragement.

Sometimes we're our own worst enemy because we want this rotten no-good sinner who's lucky to be in a relationship with us to shape up and get their act together, but we forget that the best motivation to change is not conviction but encouragement. Grace has power to change us that the law doesn't have.

Christ did not come to condemn, remember. "For God did not send his Son into the world to condemn the world" (John 3:17).

No, though our sin divorced us from God, Christ came into the world to do the supernatural work of reconciliation through atonement. He stands not as our accuser but goes to the cross as our forgiver. And in the most radical act of love ever committed in the history of the universe, the holy God of wrath pardons rebels, cancels their debts, and even commits to forgetting all their sins (Isa. 43:25; Heb. 8:12). What does this mean, except that he keeps no record of wrongs? Jesus obliterates the argument time machine.

Crazy Love

The year 1963 was a very tense one for the United States. The American people were still anxious from the Cuban Missile Crisis the year prior, and that year saw the assassination of JFK, the continuation of the Vietnam War, and rising racial tensions. On September 15 of that year one of the most heinous acts of racial terrorism in our nation's history was carried out, as White supremacists connected to the Ku Klux Klan planted a bomb underneath the front steps of 16th Street Baptist Church in downtown Birmingham, Alabama. Where would Black folks be on Sunday morning? Going to worship God.

The explosion killed four little girls and wounded twenty-two others. The four who were killed—Addie Mae Collins, Cynthia Wesley, Carole Robertson, and Carol Denise McNair—were all between the ages of eleven and fourteen, and at the time were directly under the blast, in the church basement, changing into their choir robes.

The FBI knew by 1965 who the killers were, but it took until 1977—*fourteen* years after the crime—for any prosecutions to take place. And at that point just one of the perpetrators faced trial. It took until 2002, nearly *forty* years after the murders, for the remaining killers to be sentenced.

That's a long time to wait for justice.

I remember watching a 1997 documentary from Spike Lee about the murders called *4 Little Girls*. At one point in the film, some of the families speak of having forgiven the murderers. This seems to take Lee by surprise. He is confounded. The idea that these families could forgive such a heinous and hateful act seems absolutely bewildering to him.

How could someone forgive somebody for something that terrible? Especially if they had not shown any remorse. Maybe you've wrestled with that before yourself. Maybe you're wrestling with something like that right now.

In 2013, the four girls posthumously received the Congressional Gold Medal. There had been a fifth girl in that basement getting ready for church with the others. She survived the blast that killed her friends. Her name is Sarah Rudolph. The bombing caused her catastrophic injuries, including the loss of one of her eyes. She struggles with post-traumatic stress disorder to this day. But Rudolph once said something astounding about all of this. She said, "When I would go to bed at night, I would just cry all night long, just why did they kill those girls? But being bitter won't bring the girls back, won't bring my sight back. So I had to forgive because it was what God wanted me to do."[2]

I imagine it is incredibly difficult for Sarah Rudolph to extricate herself from the time machine in her own mind. That moment likely replays inside of her often, apart from her own choosing. She is afflicted by it constantly. But she also makes a conscious commitment to drop the record of wrong. This is what forgiveness is: canceling the debt someone owes us.

When we are hurt in some way, wronged by another, our natural inclination is toward justice. And that is a good thing. It is put inside of us by God himself; the human inclination toward justice is part of what it means to be made in the image of God. But our justice is frequently imperfect. It is complicated by our fallen nature. We don't just want to see wrongs made right, we want to see wrongdoers destroyed, dehumanized. We can be bloodthirsty. This is why, even in little spats and arguments, we get so worked up beyond simply making our case and try to utterly demoralize and sometimes emotionally overwhelm our opponent. The goal isn't reconciliation or even agreement; it is conquest.

Love comes as a great interrupter. It pacifies our blood-thirst. It can soothe our nerves. It can rewire our thinking about the other person. In love, we don't want to just win the argument, we want to win *the person*. So we bring the reality of love to our consideration of past and present wrongs. We let love reframe our consideration of them. It doesn't tell us wrongs are rights! But it does give us the perspective of God's story line, a big picture vantage point about *his* glory and *his* name being known, which puts our own desire for vengeance in stunning perspective. Humbled by the portrait of God's love we see in the Scriptures, for instance, we find the supernatural strength to confront even great evils with greater mercy.

I learned something new recently as I returned to this story, something I didn't know about it previously. I discovered that the sermon scheduled to be preached the morning of September 15, 1963, when a terrorist bombing took the lives of four little girls, was titled "A Love That Forgives."

Gravity of Love

The most astonishing tale of forgiveness in the Old Testament is probably that of Joseph and his brothers. You likely remember the backstory. You know Joseph's brothers hated him with intense envy. They think first of murdering him, throwing him into a deep pit, but eventually sell him into slavery instead.

But what his brothers meant for evil, God meant for good. Joseph works his way up from slavery to great prominence in the land of Egypt, but then it all falls apart when he is falsely accused of sexual impropriety with an official's wife. Joseph is imprisoned, with the threat of death looming over him, but what this woman meant for evil, God meant for good. Joseph works his way back up to prominence again.

And then a great famine hits the land. Joseph has a great power to help those who are suffering, which, wouldn't you know it, eventually includes his murderous brothers. He plays with them a little bit, as at first they do not recognize him. But soon he is overtaken . . . by love.

You would think he'd want to kill them! He now has the power to exact vengeance, to pay these sinners back for their crimes against him. Joseph lost a lot of years in his suffering and his torment. And on top of all that, his brothers had severed him from his close relationship with his father, Jacob. Don't you think he was angry at times? In his weaker moments, he might have imagined the day he could finally face his siblings again and get his justice. But instead, "Joseph kissed each of his brothers as he wept" (Gen. 45:15).

It's an emotional scene and a healing one. Joseph brings the whole family to Egypt, including the father he misses so much. But forgiveness is so counterintuitive, those who receive it often doubt it. When Jacob dies, fear sets in. "When Joseph's brothers saw that their father was dead, they said to one another, 'If Joseph is holding a grudge against us, he will certainly repay us for all the suffering we caused him'" (50:15).

Now that Dad's dead, the brothers are wondering if all bets are off. Perhaps Joseph was only being nice to them for the sake of their father. *Now that Jacob's gone*, they're thinking, *we'll finally see the real Joseph.*

They even try to butter him up, and they attempt to play the "dear old dad" card:

> So they sent this message to Joseph, "Before he died your father gave a command: 'Say this to Joseph: Please forgive your brothers' transgression and their sin—the suffering they caused you.' Therefore, please forgive the transgression of the servants of the God of your father." (vv. 16–17)

They don't need to do this. But they are so distrustful and fearful.

Aren't they just like us?

I don't know about you, but I tend to think in these "last straw" kinds of ways. I have had trouble since as far back as I can remember believing that God would actually forgive me. It just doesn't make sense. But put to the test once again, even knowing they're lying to him about this message from Dad, what does Joseph do? He weeps (v. 17).

Joseph forgives them. Again.

This tells us the first important thing we need to know about forgiveness: it is meant to be evidence of God's grace.

Forgiveness is not when we say that what somebody did was all right but when we say that we will not hold it against them.

And this is why I think the Bible teaches that forgiveness is unilateral, a one-way action: forgiveness that proves God's grace is forgiveness that is given even when people don't deserve it.

This is what makes it so bewildering! People cannot understand this.

"You forgave them?"

"Yes."

"But they weren't sorry!"

"That's not the point. Grace was given to me when I wasn't sorry. The reality of grace means I didn't deserve it. Who am I to withhold from others what I have graciously received from God?"

I know Christians can debate this point, as some argue that you cannot forgive someone who has not repented, but I don't think forgiveness is meant to be contingent on repentance. You can forgive someone who isn't sorry. Just like you can repent of a sin someone won't forgive you for. You can't be reconciled if there's not both repentance and forgiveness—two willing parties—but you can have either of the latter so long as one responsible party is willing.

Where do we see this in the Bible?

Well, Jesus tells us to love our enemies and do good to those who hate us (Luke 6:27). He doesn't say only love those who treat us well, those who deserve it. He says to love and bless even those who are against us.

The gospel itself is a reminder of unilateral forgiveness. Jesus, on the cross, forgives those actively murdering him (23:34). "God proves his own love for us in that while we were still sinners, Christ died for us" (Rom. 5:8).

If we have been forgiven so graciously, we ought to forgive graciously (Col. 3:13).

Now, again, this does not mean we are declaring that sins committed against us are okay. Still less does it mean that forgiveness requires us to remain in abusive or otherwise harmful situations. It just means we are forgoing vengeance.

Forgiveness isn't a whitewashing of sin. Notice that Joseph clearly says in Genesis 50:20, "You planned evil against me." He's not excusing it. He's not glossing over it. He's not acting like it's no big deal. He's calling it what it is. But he's also forgiving it. There's a difference.

Charles Spurgeon once said,

> If a man has injured me, I must forgive him; and if I find him to be faulty, I must love him till he gets better, and if I cannot make him better by ordinary love, I must love him more, even as Christ loved his church and gave himself for it, "that he might present it to himself a glorious church, not having spot or wrinkle, or any such thing." He did not love her because she was without spot or wrinkle, but to get the spots and wrinkles out of her; he loved her into holiness.[3]

In the end, we forgive as an extension of the gracious forgiveness God has given us. And we forgive because we know that God's grace is doing things in the world that are bigger and better and more eternal than our need for personal satisfaction.

Forgiveness helps prove the existence of God's grace.

Love Makes the World Go 'Round

As stunning as Joseph's gracious forgiveness of his brothers is, his rationale is perhaps even more stunning. Joseph says in Genesis 50:20, "You planned evil against me; God planned it for good."

What an unbelievable thing to say! God's plans for good somehow work through others' plans for evil?

If we are forgoing vengeance, we are in effect leaving it up to God. Forgiveness is a huge step of faith, because it's a handing over of the situation to God. We hand our hurts to him, we hand our sense of justice to him, we hand our preferred outcome to him. When we forgive, we are deciding that he can be trusted to do with the offenses against us something better than we can do with them ourselves.

To forgive, for Joseph, means leaning into the sovereignty of God. And this is not the only time he's done this. Back in Genesis 45:5, during the initial reunion with his brothers, where Joseph forgives for the first time, he basically says, "God sent me through this to save lives." He knows God has a purpose for all his troubles, including the betrayal and hurt from his brothers.

Joseph has a right to be angry; he has a right to justice. After the death of his father, he has another opportunity to give way to bitterness. And he could be thinking, *You know, I didn't get much time with my dad. My brothers stole that from me. I loved my dad. And they took away my relationship with him. And after all these years, I only got to see him old and worn down and only for a little while, and now he's gone again. I missed out on so much.*

He looks down on his brothers, and he could say that all bets are off. Instead, he says, "Don't be afraid. Am I in the place of God?" (v. 19).

And he doesn't just mean in the place of God's judgment. Don't get me wrong—he *does* mean that. He does mean, "I cannot judge like God judges." But in the context—"God meant this for good"—and going back to Genesis 45, where he says to them, "God sent me here," Joseph *also* means this: "I am not in the place of control of my life."

This may be something helpful you can say every morning. Look in the mirror and say to yourself, "I am not in the place of control of my life." Or simply say this: "I am not God."

But too often we do think we're little gods. We do put ourselves in the place of God.

And then trouble comes along and reminds us, "You aren't sovereign."

Joseph has learned this hard lesson. He has wrestled with this feeling of helplessness and hopelessness in the depths of dark pits and in the dank dungeons of prisons. He's considered the evil against him from his brothers and the evil against him from Potiphar's wife. And he's come out the other side saying, "God is faithful, God is loving. God has a plan that I can't see, but I trust him, because God is sovereign. Because God is God!"

Because God is God and Joseph is not, God is sovereign and Joseph is not.

But it's only a cold comfort to know that God is sovereign if you don't also know that he's *love*. This is ultimately what Joseph is trusting. Not that God is some great puppet master doing whatever he wants with human lives out of some strange desire or for his own amusement. No, Joseph forgives because he knows that God's sovereign plan is, according to Genesis 50:20, "the survival of many people."

God's plan is not to harm his children but, in the end, to give them the hope of eternity. We can trust in his sovereignty if we will trust in his love.

Ultimately, what we see in Joseph's radical refusing to keep a record of wrongs against his brothers is a glorious picture of the good news of Jesus Christ. The whole story just fore-shadows the cross of Jesus. What Joseph is doing—by God's design, not his—is laying one more historical cobblestone in the Old Testament path that runs to the cross.

Love Is a Many Splendored Thing

In June of 2015, a young man named Dylann Roof entered a Bible study in a predominantly Black church in Charleston, South Carolina. Although they weren't accustomed to having visits from young White males, the church folks welcomed Dylann to the study and treated him warmly. And when the Bible study was over, he took out a gun and murdered nine of those in attendance. He later said he wanted his act of terrorism to incite a race war.

Less than a week later, at Roof's bond hearing, several family members of the victims expressed something the unbelieving world could not seem to wrap their minds around.

"I forgive you," said Nadine Collier, the daughter of seventy-year-old victim Ethel Lance, her voice breaking with emotion. "You took something very precious from me. I will never talk to her again. I will never, ever hold her again. But I forgive you. And have mercy on your soul."

Myra Thompson, sister of another of the victims, also said, "I acknowledge that I am very angry. But one thing that DePayne always enjoined in our family . . . is she taught me that we are the family that love built. We have no room for hating, so we have to forgive. I pray God on your soul."[4]

Maybe you followed some of his trial. If so, you know that Dylann Roof has shown zero remorse. He is a terrible human being. He opted to act in his own defense, and between his courtroom statements and his private journals we see someone undeniably and unreservedly evil. He said, "I have not shed a tear for the lives I took." He has said he doesn't regret it at all and he'd do it again if he could.

A jury found him unanimously guilty. At his sentencing, one of his victims spoke. Felicia Sanders survived the massacre, but her son did not.

> When the trial began, she described lying under a table while "bullets started flying everywhere," holding her eleven-year-old granddaughter so close that she thought she was suffocating her.
>
> When Felicia Sanders testified about her son's death, she looked directly at Roof through her tears, saying he was "refusing to look at me right now" while she described his firing five bullets into her son. . . . [S]he called Roof by his full name, telling him that he had gotten into her head. Clutching the tattered Bible she carried to the church on the night of the shooting, she said she can no longer shut her eyes to pray out of fear of another attack. But she said she can still find comfort in the torn and bloodied book she showed to the court.[5]

To Dylann Roof, who wouldn't even look at her, she said, "Yes, I forgive you."

What is happening here? These families have a right to be angry, they have a right to demand justice, but they mention "mercy." They mention "the family that love built." They mention "God [acting] on your soul." Like Joseph, these forgivers have the opportunity to demand retribution and let bitterness reign, but instead they cling to the hope of grace.

The entirety of Joseph's story—and ours, whenever we forgive—becomes one big splendid shadow cast by the cross. The cross is the place where God's wrath and mercy meet. The cross is the intersection of grace and justice, because it is at the cross where God punishes sin—pours out his wrath on the transgressions against him—and in doing so, pours out his mercy on sinners by the blood of his Son, Jesus Christ.

Like Joseph's brothers, we come to this intersection of wrath and mercy. We look up to it, knowing that we deserve to be judged and condemned. When we are convicted of our sin and know that we deserve wrath, we say, like Joseph's brothers, "Please forgive us." We are desperate for forgiveness. And the cross of Jesus Christ says to the repentant sinner: do not fear.

Joseph says, "Am I in the place of God?" Well, Jesus Christ *is* God! He *was* in the place of God. But he left the place of God behind to take on human flesh. And John 3:17 tells us that "God did not send his Son into the world to condemn the world, but to save the world through him." So the God-man, Jesus Christ, put himself in the place of sinful man, in the place of the condemned man, nailed to the cross.

The cross is the event that the Romans, the Jews, the entire world meant for evil. The cross is the outcome that Satan and his hellish schemes meant for evil. And yet despite all that, it was not some Plan B in God's sovereign design. God was not surprised by the crucifixion of his Son. No, the cross was the plan of salvation all along. The Lamb was slain from the foundation of the world (Rev. 13:8). Therefore, what Christ's killers meant for evil, God meant for good, even as Joseph says, "to bring about the present result—the survival of many people" (Gen. 50:20).

The cross of Christ is the great interrupter of human agendas. The sinful world says, "We mean this for evil," but the God of all comfort says, "Well, I mean it for good!"

Jesus died on the cross that we might be made alive. And just as Joseph's forgiveness was just the beginning of his provision and comfort for his brothers, the cross of Christ makes provision of the blood of Christ for us, for all time. We are never lacking in coverage by the blood of Christ. Its provision is eternal. And we are never lacking in comfort from the cross of Christ. Its peace is everlasting. Christians should never worry about their standing with God, because the cross is his final word that his intentions with us are characterized by kindness.

If you're ever anxious, ever doubtful, ever struggling, ever hurting, ever wounded, ever wrestling with forgiveness and repentance and reconciliation, look to the cross. The cross is proof that God loves sinners and that even the most impossible forgiveness is in fact possible.

Like Joseph's brothers, we come hemming and hawing to the cross. We sit down to our prayers and poke around the issues God most wants to deal with in us. We wonder if it could even be true that God's love could be so presumed upon. But Christ is an unending fountain of grace. His love is a many splendored thing! It surprises us, shocks us, dazzles us.

The cross declares to every weary sinner ready for the embrace of God, "It is finished." The cross in fact is proof that God is more eager to forgive than we are to sin!

What is Genesis 50 but Joseph, after all he's been through and all he's seen the work of the Lord in, resting all his hope in the promise of the grace of God? It is a picture of the gospel of Jesus Christ. The good news that God loves sinners and saves all who repent and believe in his Son.

Can you imagine this perspective Joseph had? Especially after all he's been through? Are you struggling to forgive someone? Consider how Joseph could've looked down at his brothers, those miserable losers still trying to game the system, and shaken his head. "It's always something with these guys," he could've said.

But Joseph's life with all of its ups and downs had taught him something. He learned that God is faithful, that God is sovereign, that God can be trusted. And when the crucial confrontation came, he decided, like Jesus in the garden of Gethsemane pondering the cross, "Not my will, but [God's] be done" (Luke 22:42).

St. John Chrysostom notes about Joseph that even in the recounting of his travails, he does not lash out, though he certainly could.

Even when Joseph finds it necessary to mention the cause of his imprisonment, and the reason why he was remaining there, he doesn't tell the whole story. Do you remember what he said? "For in fact I was stolen out of the land of the Hebrews; and here also I have done nothing that they should have put me into the dungeon" (Gen. 40:15). He doesn't mention the adulteress or congratulate himself on the matter, which would have been anyone's tendency to do. . . . Do you see how Joseph cares for her? Potiphar's wife did not have love for him, but evil intent. It wasn't Joseph that she loved, but she sought to fulfill her own lust. . . . But Joseph is not savage. . . . He shows the same goodwill and love toward his brothers, later in the story, who had once wanted to kill him; and then too he never says one harsh thing of them.[6]

Joseph asked himself this question: What decision would make God look biggest?

And so we see the endurance of love in Joseph's story. Over and over again, he kept no record of wrongs.

And we face these key questions too: Do I want to get payback? Or do I want to make Jesus look big?

Remember, as John Perkins says, "Forgiveness is a decision of the will. It is not a feeling."[7] Through great pain, Christ the Lord forgave us. And if he has thrown away the ledger, why don't we?

Could You Be Loved?

Love finds no joy in unrighteousness but rejoices in the truth.

1 Corinthians 13:6

I see people who are supposed to know better standin' around like furniture. There's a wall between you and what you want and you got to leap it.

Bob Dylan[1]

I don't love you anymore."

I blinked slowly. I turned the declaration over in my mind. It slid slowly down into my heart like sludge through a drain. After a whole life spent looking for love, it had come to this.

I could not say I didn't see it coming. The clues were there all along. I had been hardening my wife's heart against me for years. This was the rotten fruit of my own sin now blossoming before me.

My sin of choice for years was pornography, and it poisoned everything. Trying to keep it a secret only worked for so long. Seeds had been planted in the fifth grade, when a classmate brought one of his dad's *Penthouse* magazines onto the school bus. The graphic images snagged into my brain and didn't let go. My lustful appetites were triggered then, starving for satisfaction that would always elude me, though I tried and tried to appease them in later years with my secret shame.

I got my first computer when I was a freshman in college. Still living at home then, I nevertheless spent hours in my room. The snail's pace of dial-up internet could not dissuade me. I was feeding a monster whose hunger could not be satisfied. And I carried this, unbeknownst to Becky, into our marriage.

Porn rewires the brain. Worse than that, it quenches the Spirit. Outwardly I feverishly tried to maintain the look of a good Christian kid, managing my image and massaging my reputation. I tried to look smart, humble, godly. But I was being eaten alive. Everything that spiritual and emotional maturity entails—the ability to delay gratification, the true humility of selflessness, the exhibition of kindness and gentleness, the exercise of self-control—was stunted by my repetitive sin.

The thing about ravenous lust is that you might be able to keep it secret, but you can't keep it private. It outs itself in a million ways. I was selfish, rude, and short-tempered. It's not pornography's fault. That blame belonged to me. The manifestation of it could've easily been alcohol or drugs or some other secret sin, but the depravity began inside of me.

And after ten years, long enough to learn that my pleas for forgiveness and promises to do better were all empty, Becky was done being had.

"I don't love you anymore. You're not the person I thought you were."

She had finally realized that the hidden me was the real me, and she was done helping me pretend. She was, in fact, *done*.

What I didn't know—what she didn't know—is that her declaration of lovelessness in that moment was itself an act of love. She did not feel that then, or even think it. But it was exactly what I needed.

The truth is that she didn't feel love for me—I had obliterated that possibility—but she was, in a very strange way, despite even her intentions, loving me by telling me she didn't love me. It woke me up. Even if she didn't mean it this way, it was for my good and glory.

But I'm getting ahead of myself.

To All the Girls I've Loved Before

That playacted wedding ceremony with my first grade sweetheart in the giant wooden shoe was just the epicenter of my infatuation with love, which, as I look back, was really an infatuation with *feeling* loved—or what I thought feeling loved was. After Elizabeth and I were unceremoniously divorced by the circumstances of more playground crushes and simply "moving on," I embarked throughout my childhood on a journey to recapture over and over again my own self-centered vision of love.

There was Stella, the first girl I ever got in a fight over. My buddy Jansen and I legitimately got into fisticuffs because we both thought she should be ours. As it happened, Stella wasn't interested in either one of us. But I was already off to the races conceiving of love as personal conquest.

There was Lucy, my fifth grade girlfriend. Blonde-haired and blue-eyed, she lived in my neighborhood, and we'd play soccer in the cul-de-sac or wander around our homes holding hands. She was my first slow dance. It was to Brian Adams's "Heaven" at a friend's party. As I think about it now, some thirty-five years later, I shudder to think of my own kids slow dancing at that age! Where were my friend's parents? What a parental nightmare! But it felt like a dream to me. I was "in love."

I remember when I first asked Lucy to "go around" (our phrase for the dating we weren't old enough to do). I slipped a note into her cubby at school. It literally said, "Do you want to go around with me? Check yes or no." And then I added a cruel postscript: "You have to stop sucking your thumb." Yes, my dear Lucy was a ten-year-old thumb-sucker, and as outgrown of that as she should have been, it was mean of me to make it a contingency of my affections. I was a little relational legalist, making my love conditional on her performance. *You are not worthy of me*, I was unwittingly saying to her. But she did stop, and we became one of the class couples, subject to both the admiration and the teasing this status inevitably entailed.

After Lucy, I pursued a series of adolescent girlfriends. Kenzie in junior high. Marla, Jennifer, and Hillary in high school. There were many unrequited loves as well, but the ones who deigned to be associated with me simply became outlets for my own narcissistic romanticism.

What was I really searching for in all of these immature romances? I don't think it's anything unusual. I think it was what we all want deep down, even into our adulthood. I could not have identified it at the time, or even expressed it if I could, but I was after that high of "feeling loved." In my insidest insides, what I really wanted was to feel okay, to feel accepted, to feel wanted, to feel validated.

This is probably more information than you want—please forgive me—but I was always a neurotic kid, very timid and uncomfortable in my own skin. I was reasonably good at academics and at sports, so I managed to fit in fairly well in most school pecking orders, only occasionally subject to bullying and occasionally being a bully myself, but throughout it all, I just pretty much hated myself and thought if I could get someone to love me, I might finally feel normal. It never worked.

I was a stutterer from kindergarten and struggled with this speech impediment all the way into college. This only exacerbated my lack of confidence and sense of dis-ease in the world. Even more exacerbating was growing up in a church culture that was grace-deficient. I always attended churches that preached the biblical gospel, but they seemed to save it only for special occasions, and even then, only for lost people. Several times throughout my adolescence, I wondered if I was even saved. I think now that those moments of doubt were the only explanations I could find for why I felt so unloved. *Maybe I don't actually know God,* I'd think.

Discipleship for me was conducted in one performance-based culture after another. Grace seemed elusive, stingy. I had a tape that played in my head since as long as I can remember that basically said, on repeat, "You're only as good as what you haven't done." As good as I could be in school or on the playground or even in church, it was never quite good enough. I was keenly aware of my own inadequacies, and certainly of most of my own sin, but I could not fathom the idea of a God who loved me as I was, whose Son died for me and accepted me as I was. My conception of love was a mess, because my perception of God was a mess.

When I met Becky, I felt like I had finally found someone who "got me," who loved me for me. And she did. But I was still playing the game. And she was so rich with grace, it was easy to spend it. Finally feeling accepted, finally feeling loved, I put my own love on autopilot. Turned in on my own self, I added laziness about love to my own sins.

And then there was my secret sin, always crouching at the door waiting to devour me. Eventually it devoured us both.

Ten years in, she'd reached her limit. She had to protect herself from the hurt I was unwilling to stop.

Love Hurts

Paul says in 1 Corinthians 13:6, "Love finds no joy in un-righteousness but rejoices in the truth." There are a hundred ways to take this. The primary way, of course, is that love does not celebrate wrongdoing or immorality. Love is opposed to sin. To "rejoice in the truth" is to enjoy the reality of God and his gospel. But it also means doing the hard work of speaking hard words, especially when unrighteousness is at hand.

Sometimes loving someone doesn't feel like love to them.

My first encounter with Graham Greene's brilliant story *The End of the Affair* was in reviewing the Neil Jordan film adaptation for my college newspaper. I was obsessed with movies about adultery then, for some reason. I even wrote a piece for the university literary magazine analyzing the different portrayals of affairs in Woody Allen's *Hannah and Her Sisters* and other films. If I had to psychoanalyze myself, I would say I was subconsciously working out my lustful betrayal of my own marriage. I had not cheated on my wife with another woman, but I essentially had with countless women on a computer or video screen.

I hated *The End of the Affair* film. There was a spirit of something intriguing there about faith and disbelief, but the whole thing seemed muted, hazy, smeared over with the maudlin romanticism so common in Hollywood period pieces. Someone later convinced me to pick up the source material, however, and I discovered in Greene's work, the fourth of his more explicitly Christian novels, what could not be captured on-screen: the often maddening complexities of belief and disbelief, and the thin line between raging against God and fearing him. This dynamic touched something deeper in me, perhaps even planting a seed for my later awakening and repentance.

"A story has no beginning or end," Greene's story begins.[2] There is something else that has no beginning or end—or Someone else, rather, and his shadow looms large over each page of the novel, which chronicles the adulterous affair between writer Maurice Bendrix and Sarah Miles, the wife of a British officer.

The illicit romance seems routine enough: passionate artist type woos the bored wife of a boring man. But during one of their encounters a bomb blast during the German blitzkrieg of London destroys their room, nearly killing Maurice. After this traumatic event, the romance mysteriously sours, and Maurice is sent into a tailspin of jealousy and lust.

He believes he's been traded in for a new lover, so he hires a private investigator who discovers that indeed Maurice has been replaced. But Sarah's new lover turns out to be the Source of all love himself. When Maurice nearly died, Sarah prayed for his safety and made a deal with God: if her lover's life was spared, she would cut off their affair. As painful as it was to give up her illicit dalliance, the alternative was more painful. She feared not for body first but for soul. And here we find something rather strange and unique in the great midst of literary exploration of sexual sin. Where so many romantic works treat adultery as "natural," totally legitimized by Romance, the great theoretical justifier of all things, here is a little book where the woman loves her lover by *not* "loving" him.

It is never loving, of course, to engage in sin. (This is why, for instance, I even hate the word *affair* to this day. That word rhetorically romanticizes what the Bible condemns.) Sarah knew it would break Maurice's heart to stop committing adultery with him, but breaking his heart was finally the first act of loving him she had committed!

Sometimes love hurts. We see this not just in extreme examples, as in Greene's novel, but also in the "tough love" parents exhibit with children on a daily basis in the setting of boundaries or exercising of discipline, or even in the extreme examples of "cutting off" or otherwise refusing to enable prodigal children. And we see it formally in the biblical exercise of church discipline, when a congregation's commitment to the faith and to faithful public witness leads them to remove an unbeliever from membership.

We have to be careful with tough love, of course. As I said in a previous chapter, abusers are often keen to call their sinful harshness "love." But real love refuses to rejoice in unrighteousness. It rejoices in the truth. And sometimes *the truth* hurts. As Leon Morris writes, "Love is never harsh, but it can be stern."[3]

Of course, Sarah's ending of the relationship infuriates the worldly Maurice, who comes to see religion itself as another boring husband dampening all his romantic fervor, frustrating the artistic expression of his very appetites. And when Sarah later contracts tuberculosis and dies, he sees her God not just as an interloper but as a villain. God is the big spoilsport, the dasher of lustful hopes.

And that is where Greene's tale really deepens. In her withholding, in her painful disengagement, and now in her cruel death, Sarah has taught Maurice more about love than she ever could have in the immoral passion of their previous life together. And Maurice is now forced for the first time to reckon with the great enemy of his fleshly appetites, the great unbounded Author who had so unfairly deleted his story.

I am reminded of C. S. Lewis's line about his youthful atheism: "I maintained that God did not exist," he said. "I was also very angry with God for not existing."[4] Indeed, in the end, as Maurice shakes his fist at Sarah's God, rejecting the object of her prayers on his behalf, proclaiming defiantly even his hatred for God—"I wanted Sarah for a lifetime and You took her away. With Your great schemes You ruin our happiness like a harvester ruins a mouse's nest: I hate You, God, I hate You as though You existed"[5]—we think he doth protest too much. He doesn't even seem to realize he's praying.

No, being angry with God is not right or just. But it's a start. When the story ends, Maurice's Jacob-like wrestling is just beginning. We are sure, by the last lines, gleaming with a sliver of hope like a light through a cracked door—"I said to Sarah, all right, have it your way. I believe you live and that He exists"[6]—that Maurice will not walk away from his wrestling unchanged. The reader walks away, in fact, with the great hope that hatred may have a peculiar advantage over ambivalence in that it is at least a kind of caring, a passion that is simply waiting for the redirection of the transforming gospel.

This is a lot like what happened to me that horrible, wonderful day my wife said she didn't love me anymore.

Love Rescue Me

When you are at the end of yourself, you pray differently. After Becky's announcement, I was crushed, undone. What

I should have seen at so many points before in her painful pleadings, I suddenly and climactically saw in living color. It was over. I banished myself to the guest bedroom, where I spent about a year in emotional darkness, the threat of divorce always looming over me.

It was the worst period of my life. But I deserved every second of it (and more). It was what it took. But I didn't know all that at the time. I just knew I was desperate and empty and, worst of all, unloved. And I had no one to blame but myself.

I struggled constantly with thoughts of suicide. This was the other extreme of my narcissism. Now that its previous outlet—the use of my wife—was ended, I turned it in on myself. Serious depression set in, messing with my mind.

My depression was a kind of funhouse mirror, exaggerating little things and minimizing big ones. My thoughts were inverted. I heard constantly the voice of the Enemy telling me that since it was all over, I might as well end it for real. Who could love me? Who would want me now? I could in fact finally prove my love by removing myself from the earth, subtracting myself from the orbit of the one I hurt. She could finally know I really loved her if I punished myself this way. (For many of those days, it did not occur to me that this would be the worst hurt of all. I was too wrapped up in myself even then to think straight.)

I stared death in the face constantly. I surfed "painless suicide" message boards online. Driving home from men's Bible studies, during which I still worked hard to maintain the façade of being put together, I often had to force myself not to veer my car off the road and into the trees lining the winding highway between church and home. A few times I sat in the darkened garage, an extension cord in my hands, contemplating the beams on the ceiling.

Look, I wanted out. I had dashed my own dreams, to be sure; I knew I needed to be punished, but I felt totally helpless, utterly hopeless.

At night, lying facedown on the floor of that guest bedroom, wetting the carpet with my tears, I would hear the CD of lullabies playing on repeat in my daughter's room across the hall. Michael Card would sing "Sleep Sound in Jesus." He was reminding me that the Lord was watching over me. But I barely believed it.

Until one night. I don't remember the date. But I remember vividly what happened. I was on the floor, begging God to help me, asking him to let me go. I was asking him to do something, anything, I don't know exactly what, but to end my pain, to end my agony. I was praying a groaning, one-word prayer over and over: "Please . . . please . . . please." And something extraordinary happened. I felt as though the hand of God himself reached into that room and took hold of me. And I heard him say—not audibly, but clearly still—*I love you.*

It wasn't anything I hadn't heard before, but it was as if I had never heard it before. A light came on inside of me. A supernatural power came over me.

What did I discover at that moment?

It was what I had been looking for all my life.

When I was at the point of most wanting to check out, to give up, to give in—when I felt completely abandoned and totally alone and entirely unloved—I believed against belief, hoped against hope that Christ was there with me. "Yea, though I walk through the valley of the shadow of death, I will fear no evil: for thou art with me" (Ps. 23:4 KJV).

I had come to the end of my rope and found there the sufficiency of Christ. I brokenly submitted to the reality that my life was in his hands, not my own. I came to the end of myself and found there the goodness of Jesus. It is a great irony of life this side of the veil that we see the loveliness of Christ more brightly the lower we get. And he'd been with me all along. When I felt most alone, in fact he was closer than ever. As John Flavel says, "He looks down from heaven upon all my afflictions, and understands them more fully than I that feel them."[7]

Martin Luther describes the experience this way:

> They who are tormented with high spiritual temptations, which every one is not able to endure, should have this example before their eyes, when they are in sorrow and heaviness of spirit, fearing God's wrath, the day of judgment, and everlasting death, and such like fiery darts of the devil. Let them comfort themselves, that although they often feel such intolerable sufferings, yet are they never the more rejected of God, but are of him better beloved.[8]

I had been plunged into the depths of despair and, by God's grace, found myself simultaneously plunged into the true depth of the gospel. Everything I'd desired had ended, except what I was stupidly looking for in the wrong places: the satisfying grace of God. Stripped down to nothing but need, I came face-to-face with grace. I was at my worst, and the holy God of the universe loved me anyway.

Because of that moment, to this day I feel powerfully in my bones the truth of Romans 8:38–39:

> For I am persuaded that neither death nor life, nor angels nor rulers, nor things present nor things to come, nor powers, nor height nor depth, nor any other created thing will be able to separate us from the love of God that is in Christ Jesus our Lord.

Christian, this is eternally true for you too. You may never go through what I did, or you may go through worse— perhaps you already have—but you must fight the devil's temptation to doubt the reality of true love. The promises of Jesus are good. They are real. And they are worth living for, no matter your pain or predicament.

Jesus will never reject you, ever.

I love the reflection of old Puritan John Bunyan on John 6:37, pondering all the reasons we can come up with that may negate Christ's promise about us:

> "But I am an old sinner," you say. "I will in no wise cast out," says Christ.
>
> "But I am a hard-hearted sinner," you say. "I will in no wise cast out," says Christ.
>
> "But I am a backsliding sinner," you say. "I will in no wise cast out," says Christ.
>
> "But I have served Satan all my days," you say. "I will in no wise cast out," says Christ.
>
> "But I have sinned against light," you say. "I will in no wise cast out," says Christ.

"But I have sinned against mercy," you say. "I will in no wise cast out," says Christ.

"But I have no good thing to bring with me," you say. "I will in no wise cast out," says Christ.[9]

He "will never leave you nor forsake you" (Heb. 13:5 ESV). Do you want true love? It is eternally ever yours, in him.

Let Love Be Your Energy

Feeling loved often makes us more loving people, doesn't it? Similarly, knowing the love of Christ in the gospel transforms us, as the Spirit indwells our hearts, into people who gradually learn to love as Christ loves. As the old hymn goes,

> My song is love unknown,
> My Savior's love to me;
> Love to the loveless shown,
> That they might lovely be.[10]

I was supernaturally able to "be lovely" when I supernaturally encountered the loveliness of Christ.

When that moment I call "gospel wakefulness" occurred, my circumstances did not miraculously change. Becky's feelings toward me did not change. But the joy that came over me prepared me and energized me to love like I never had before, to truly love. How do I know? I spent months thereafter loving my wife with no hope of its return. The consequences of sin did not abate. And this is how you know you truly love: you orient yourself toward another for their good and glory without requiring reciprocation.

It was a small price to pay compared to her loving me with no return for an entire decade.

Every morning I got up, aware of the profound brokenness in our relationship, able with God's help to acknowledge I had created this wreckage but empowered to be a different person, to be a different *lover*.

It all culminated one Friday morning, months later. Before she left for work, Becky reiterated what I'd gradually grown to accept. She said, "I want you to move out."

I was stunned. But, strangely, I wasn't devastated. I asked if I could have the weekend, and if she still felt the same way on Monday, I would comply with her request. She said okay.

After she left, I prayed all morning. I called my father to ask for advice and get some counsel. At lunchtime, Becky called me. My hands trembling, I picked up the phone. I don't remember everything she said, but I remember this part clearly. She said, "Look, I don't want you to leave. I don't know what's happened, but I know you're different. I know you've changed. And I'm willing to figure out what we do from here."

I was overjoyed.

Now, things didn't become great overnight. It took a very long time, actually, to piece back together what I had broken. A lot of trust needed to be rebuilt, and the residual pain of my sin reverberated for years afterward. But for the first time, we were on the same page. We wanted the same thing. As hard as it might be to climb out of the pit, she wanted to do it together. We needed counseling, we argued, we had periods of distrust and returning pain—but slowly, surely, bit by bit, the Lord began to knit us back together.

As of my writing this, we've been married twenty-four years. Neither one of us could say we are where we are without the grace of God. We have an awe about the gospel of grace today that we would not have if our past had been different.

You don't know what love is until you really know who you're loving. Sin and all. And you don't know what love is until you really know the One who loves us perfectly. Despite our sin. Despite it all.

The wonder we get to know now is how to share this love with each other. This is another way of "rejoicing with the truth." Paul doesn't just mean that telling the hard truth is an act of love. He also means that loving hard people *is* rejoicing in the truth of the gospel. This gospel tells us that God loves sinners. He absolutely, weirdly, eternally loves them. The cross where his Son died is the utmost proof of this.

And because of the grace of that love, we can find the grace to love each other. "We love," John writes, "because he first loved us" (1 John 4:19).

8

How Deep Is Your Love?

[Love] bears all things, believes all things, hopes all things, endures all things.

1 Corinthians 13:7

For one human being to love another human being: that is perhaps the most difficult task that has been entrusted to us, the ultimate task, the final test and proof, the work for which all other work is merely preparation.

Rainer Maria Rilke[1]

My wife asked me a tricky question the other day. She said, "Who is your best friend?"

She meant *besides herself*, of course. What man in my life would I consider my best friend?

It's tricky because men don't tend to think of friendships in that way—best, second best, and so on. It's also tricky because I've had many men I've considered friends over the years but only a handful I'd consider *close*. When I think of a best friend, I guess I think of someone you tell almost everything to, not just someone you spend a lot of time with or with whom you share a lot in common.

I think of Eric, who was undoubtedly my best friend in high school. We were the best man in each other's weddings. After thirtysome years, we still chat probably every other week, even though we haven't lived in the same state for at least that long. Eric and I have seen each other at our worst. And we're still friends. That's something special, I think.

I also think of Bill. He's a few years older than me, and I've known him for about as long as I've known Eric. For some reason, Bill was the only friend I talked to when I was in that depressed state and wanted to end things.

David and Sarah have been close friends to Becky and me since our church planting days. They were on our leadership team, and we've stayed tight for almost twenty years now. They're younger than us, and in a lot of ways we discipled them in the early days of our friendship, but they have also counseled us in our difficult days. The students have become the teachers. David holds me accountable and asks hard questions.

Mike was my first mentor in ministry, really. He was the minister who married Becky and me, and he was the one we reached out to first for counseling when things were falling apart. We still connect regularly, as he is an influential father in the faith to me.

These men and a few others have, for all intents and purposes, "endured all things" with me. That makes them my "best friends," I guess.

The hardest part about getting older, actually, is discovering who your real friends are. This is especially true in ministry. I have experienced the deep heartbreak of encouragers becoming critics and colleagues becoming gossipers, as those I thought close stabbed me in the back.

We do friendship weirdly. Since the dawn of Facebook, when "friend" became a verb as well as a noun, things have gotten a little sideways. I remember when I resigned from my last pastorate I watched slack-jawed as church members "unfriended" me on the site. It shouldn't have hurt, but it did.

But social media didn't start this mess. We started it in Genesis 3. We once had perfect peace, *shalom*, with each other and with all creation. And we screwed it all up by trying to exalt ourselves.

Friendship is a great means of flourishing for the soul, but only if we do it right. A friend who is self-involved is not a friend at all. Takers make bad friends. And when the taken-advantage-of givers don't want to run the risk of losing the illusion of that friendship, the takers are emboldened.

Paul says love "bears all things, believes all things, hopes all things, endures all things" (1 Cor. 13:7). As with most portions of this love chapter, I suppose this could be applied in all sorts of situations.

What does it mean to believe all things and hope all things? It might mean that love gives the benefit of the doubt. Love doesn't jump to conclusions. Love advocates, rather than accuses.

What does it mean to bear all things and endure all things? Perhaps to help others shoulder their burdens, to take up one's cross in order to love those who are hard to love. I think sometimes it means pushing through conflict to actually love another person. It might mean taking the risk of "being real" to ensure your relationship isn't based on a lie.

Love on the Rocks

I lost a good friend once by confronting him about his sin. I learned then that you can lose a friend by being a friend. In the beginning of the confrontation, I wanted to "believe all things" in the sense that he would receive me fairly and hear me out. At the end of it, I had come to see the need to "bear all things" and to "endure all things."

Friendship can be weird. But it is also wonderful.

Let's chart the life of a biblical friendship together by looking at a particular conflict depicted across a few passages. We begin on one of Paul's missionary journeys:

> But Paul and Barnabas, along with many others, remained in Antioch, teaching and proclaiming the word of the Lord.

173

After some time had passed, Paul said to Barnabas, "Let's go back and visit the brothers and sisters in every town where we have preached the word of the Lord and see how they're doing." Barnabas wanted to take along John who was called Mark. But Paul insisted that they should not take along this man who had deserted them in Pamphylia and had not gone on with them to the work. They had such a sharp disagreement that they parted company, and Barnabas took Mark with him and sailed off to Cyprus. But Paul chose Silas and departed, after being commended by the brothers and sisters to the grace of the Lord. He traveled through Syria and Cilicia, strengthening the churches. (Acts 15:35–41)

This is an interesting place to start, at the seeming end of a friendship, but I want to use this moment from the ministry lives of Paul and Barnabas to track back to the beginning of their relationship and see the life of their friendship.

After his conversion experience on the road to Damascus, Paul the repentant persecutor naturally sought inclusion in the church. As a God-ordained apostle, this was especially necessary! But also naturally, the congregations were wary of this man who had spent years hating and attacking them. Enter Barnabas:

When [Paul] arrived in Jerusalem, he tried to join the disciples, but they were all afraid of him, since they did not believe he was a disciple. Barnabas, however, took him and brought him to the apostles and explained to them how Saul had seen the Lord on the road and that the Lord had talked to him, and how in Damascus he had spoken boldly in the name of Jesus. (9:26–27)

I can totally imagine what this felt like. Can you? Have you ever had a friend who had your back?

I also know what it feels like *not* to have this kind of friend. Don't you?

What was it about Paul that convinced Barnabas? Convinced him enough to vouch for him? I think there's an extraordinary grace at work here, and it is found in the kind of love that believes all things and hopes all things. This is the kind of love that prepares us to bear all things and endure all things.

Love Can Build a Bridge

All friendship is a gift of grace. This is true even for non-Christian friendships. It's true for friendships between unbelievers, between Muslims and Mormons and atheists or anybody. Friendship is itself a gift from God, a common grace. Friendship isn't something only Christians enjoy. Friendship is like coffee or classical music or the sunrise: something God made to be part of the wonder of his creation. Thus, friendship isn't distinctly a Christian thing but a human thing.

And yet friendships don't start apart from God's sovereign direction. We talk about people "making friends" all the time, but when you're really friends with someone, you didn't really *make* that friendship, did you? Doesn't friendship just kind of . . . happen?

"When David had finished speaking with Saul, Jonathan was bound to David in close friendship, and loved him as much as he loved himself" (1 Sam. 18:1). The soul of Jonathan "was bound" to the soul of David. Did they do that?

Did they bind their souls together? How do you bind your soul to someone else's?

You don't.

There is a chemistry to friendship, is there not? There's a uniqueness to friendship. That's why you're not friends with hundreds of people (except online, where you're constantly trying to figure out how to silence nearly all of them).

I don't think anybody can really be friends with very many people. The experience is too special, too unique.

We can be a friend to lots of people. We can and should be friendly to nearly everybody. But there's a difference between *to* and *with*. We can all be a friend *to* anybody. But we can't all be friends *with* everybody.

This was even true of Jesus. He had, of course, his disciples, the Twelve. But even within those twelve, he seemed to have a special intimacy with Peter, James, and John. And even then, he seemed to have a special friendship further still with John, who is sometimes singled out as "the disciple he loved" (John 13:23; 19:26; 20:2).

Well, didn't he love them all? Yes, of course, but there was something special about the relationship between him and a few.

In *The Four Loves*, C. S. Lewis famously describes friendship this way:

Friendship arises out of mere Companionship when two or more of the companions discover that they have in common some insight or interest or even taste which the others do not share and which, till that moment, each believed to be his own unique treasure (or burden). The typical expression of opening Friendship would be something like, "What? You too? I thought I was the only one."[2]

But friendship is deeper than simply sharing a common interest. Lewis is talking about something unique to the few people in the friendship. He's not talking about finding a club for your hobby or an online community that shares your interests. He's talking about finding those one or two people whose souls seem knit to your own. "There is a friend who stays closer than a brother" (Prov. 18:24). It's the kind who seems especially fit to believe, bear, and endure alongside you.

The friend that sticks closer than a brother is the one who believes and hopes all things and bears and endures all things. Something extraordinary happens in that shared experience—a shared personality. It's like lightning in a bottle or a spark, if you will. You just "click" with somebody, and the feeling is mutual.

Let me tell you a little more about my friend Bill. He's about ten years older than me, and he was a youth leader at my church when I was in high school. One summer while coming back from youth camp in a very hot van, driving from Colorado to Houston, Bill and I read through the book of Acts together. Now, that may not sound like such a great time to you, but it was exhilarating in the moment for us. We look back at that van ride home often. It was when our friendship was forged, by God's grace. And we've been friends now for a long time. He was one of the only guys I talked to about my depression and my marriage trouble back when I was going through them, because Bill is a friend who sticks closer than a brother.

Paul and Barnabas seemed to have this kind of friendship that was forged by God's grace, beginning with Barnabas sticking up for Paul, and it started one of the greatest missionary companionships in church history. In Acts 13:2–3, we read, "the Holy Spirit said, 'Set apart for me Barnabas and Saul for the work to which I have called them.' Then after they had fasted, prayed, and laid hands on them, they sent them off."

The missionaries went to Cyprus and Antioch and Iconium and Lystra and all over the place together. The Bible says they preached boldly wherever they went.

In Lystra, Paul was dragged out of the city by a mob hostile to the gospel, and they tried to stone him to death. We don't get many details on his recovery, but they assumed he was dead so we can't imagine that he just had a few rocks thrown at him. No, he was badly hurt, near death. And the next thing we read is that "the disciples gathered around him, [and] he got up and went into the town" (14:20).

What? That sounds crazy. How could a near-death Paul just get back up and march back into the city? A miraculous healing was performed, maybe. But also we note the presence of the disciples gathering around him. His friends were there. And the very next sentence says, "The next day he left with Barnabas for Derbe" (v. 20).

Their friendship continued, and it was carried on in the grace of God to fulfill the mission of God. And this is a very important point about Christian friendships we ought to remember. It is where many friendships between Christians fall apart. Christian friendships are driven by a shared mission.

Love on Display

A gospel friendship is a friendship centered on God's grace. There's common grace friendship, which almost anyone can have, and then there's a gospel friendship, which only exists when two people allow the love of Jesus to shape, inform, and define their relationship. A gospel friendship is a friendship directed by the grace of God in the gospel.

This is why the best friendships, honestly, should take place inside the church. Church folks are extraordinary sinners, to be sure. It's not like becoming a Christian means becoming not a sinner. But it means the grace of God becomes the dominating factor in our lives, and we are constantly making space for it. People in the church are to be honest in the light of God's holiness about their sins (and flaws and failings) and bold in the light of God's grace about their freedom and joy. Christian friends aren't just friends—they are eternal family. I will say much more about this in chapter 10, but for now, it's enough to make the case that the deepest friendships are those that are created and shaped by grace. These are the kinds of friendships where love is on ultimate display, because they point to the good news of God's love in Jesus.

In the beginning of Acts 15, a big dispute boils over between the circumcising party and the apostles of the gospel. This is a fight Paul will wage constantly in his ministry— against legalists, against Judaizers, against Pharisaical Christianity. This heresy is the primary target of his anger in his letter to the Galatians. This compromise of the gospel incenses Paul, drives him crazy.

So these false teachers show up and say, "Unless you get circumcised, you can't be a Christian." They are basically saying that you can't be a Christian unless you also become a Jew.

I've seen this exact thing put strains on relationships. A coworker of mine once had a friend who was not ethnically

Jewish but as a Christian had somehow decided she needed to adopt many Jewish customs, including adherence to the dietary law and observance of Jewish holidays. This woman was convinced not just that these practices could enhance her own followship of Jesus but that this was what all faithful Christians must do. She in effect became a "Judaizer." She was constantly pressuring her friend, my coworker, to join her in these observances, always suggesting she wasn't spiritual enough or obedient enough. Their friendship began to fracture. Why? Because it had become dominated by the law, not the gospel. It slowly ceased to be a gospel friendship; it ceased to be a loving one.

That's obviously a literal example of legalism severing a friendship, but we've all experienced other kinds of relational legalism, haven't we? When someone makes their love conditional upon our performance, our agreement, our satisfying their preferences, we end up in a transactional relationship that runs counter to 1 Corinthians 13 love.

The apostles in Acts 15 discussed the matters before them, and each kind of takes a turn disputing and refuting the idea that anybody gets saved by becoming Jewish. Peter gives a heartfelt response, stumping for the inclusion of the gentiles and arguing for salvation by grace alone. James says a few words. And they all listen to Paul and Barnabas recount the tales of their missionary adventures.

I am picturing this scene. Peter and James are testifying, but when Paul and Barnabas start recounting their ministry experiences, I wonder if it sounds less like a sermon and more like two bros reminiscing.

"Hey, remember when we preached at Lystra? Man, they tried to kill you, dude!"

"I know! What about that time that guy was healed in Antioch?"

"Dude, that was cuh-razy, bro!"

They are friends centered on God's grace.

And when the apostles determine to send their official encouragement and response to the gentiles to let them know that even though the legalists are harassing them, the church leaders stand behind them (Acts 15:22–31), they pick a team to do it that's led by—who else?—Paul and Barnabas.

These two guys had so experienced grace, so loved grace, so enjoyed grace, were so committed to grace that their friendship was defined by the mission of grace.

It's important in the church to understand what this really means. We suppose sometimes that grace means we ought to be friends with everybody. That's simply impossible. Remember, grace means we can be a friend *to* everybody, but it doesn't mean we can be friends *with* everybody, if only for the fact that we aren't omnipotent people. We don't have the resources or the power to be in intimate relationships with everybody.

Everyone's capacity is different, of course. Women seem to have a greater capacity for close friends than men. This capacity isn't endless, but it's not uncommon for a woman's close friendship circle to include four or five women. That's not unheard of with men, but men typically have only one or two close friends, if any. (Less a friendship circle and more a friendship triangle!)

But no matter how many close friends you have, there is a limit, right? If you have friends, the kind whose souls are knit to yours, it's just a few. Maybe one. And that's okay.

See, one of the problems in our misunderstanding of grace and our misunderstanding of friendship in the church is that we think because grace is true and powerful, Christians are obligated to be friends with anyone who wants to be friends with them. And you can be a friend to such people, but you probably can't be friends with such people, because friendship isn't negotiated or arranged by an agreement; it's made. It's forged. It "happens."

This is why, actually, people who place extraordinary burdens on the idea of friendship rarely make good friends. Love, as Paul says, "is not self-seeking" (1 Cor. 13:5).

Barnabas was an encourager. Paul was a firebrand. They complemented each other well and had a shared goal, and while their relationship began with Barnabas helping Paul in a time of great need, their friendship was not built based on just one of them needing the other to sustain him. There was a mutuality there. A back and forth. A partnership. A kinship.

I think we should be honest about the way friendship is really forged. Because I see this happen a lot in the church where someone is constantly complaining about not having friends. One of the worst ways to find friends is to be complaining about not having them. And then, when someone gets their target locked on somebody, thinking *This person needs to be my friend*, any kind of relationship that ensues isn't built on the gospel. It's built on law: you provide me with the friendship that I need to be happy.

When a person who is an emotional vacuum requests—oh, let's be honest: when they passive-aggressively *demand*—friendship, they are not positioning themselves as a potential friend but as a patient. They are not looking for a friend but a therapist, a supplier, a functional savior. They are making an invitation to codependency, not friendship.

And to be clear, again, you can be a friend *to* this person. But it is not likely you can be friends *with* them. It's hard to be friends with "takers." An emotionally needy person looking for their functional savior does not make a good friend because they reflect the demands of the law, not the gifts of the gospel.

That said, while a real friendship is not predicated on neediness, a real friend is not someone who never needs you! When my friend is hurting, grieving, or going through some other difficulty, I certainly don't feel like they've stopped being my friend. I don't feel put out or impatient with them. I don't suddenly feel as though they are inconvenient. And I think I don't feel that way precisely because *they're my friend*!

I sometimes wonder if we ought to look at friendships as a kind of covenant, somewhat like a marriage covenant. A covenant is predicated on grace, on mutual giving. Sometimes one party is weaker and must "take." But the relationship originates in a two-way giving: of time, of respect, of interests, of laughter, of help, of C. S. Lewis's celebrated "me too!"-ness.

In this way, friendships founded on real love for each other become pictures of the gospel. But as great as these friendships are, as life-giving and soul-stirring as they can be, they never, ever can replace our need for the realest thing.

Your Love Is a Miracle

Something happens in Paul and Barnabas's friendship. After they deliver the letter to the gentiles in Antioch, the rest of the team leaves but Paul and Barnabas stay to preach. Later, when Paul wants to move on, Barnabas agrees and suggests they take a fellow by the name of John Mark with them.

> Barnabas wanted to take along John who was called Mark. But Paul insisted that they should not take along this man who had deserted them in Pamphylia and had not gone on with them to the work. They had such a sharp disagreement that they parted company, and Barnabas took Mark with him and sailed off to Cyprus. But Paul chose Silas and departed, after being commended by the brothers and sisters to the grace of the Lord. (Acts 15:37–40)

We aren't told what Paul and Barnabas said to each other. We aren't told how heated it got. But it wasn't a minor disagreement. It was a "sharp disagreement."

Paul, we assume, is skittish about John Mark, mainly because during one of their previous missionary outings, he abandoned the work. Maybe Paul thought he was a quitter and couldn't be trusted. Barnabas, ever the encourager, wants to give someone another chance, right? Maybe he said to Paul, "Hey, I vouched for you when nobody wanted to give you a chance. Maybe return the favor to Mark." I imagine Paul might not have liked that.

Whatever words were actually exchanged, they were enough to sever their partnership.

Sometimes friendships go through changes. Sometimes friendships end. But if the gospel was ever present, the spirit of the gospel remains.

As far as we know, Paul and Barnabas never see each other again. They both carry on missionary lives separate from each other. Paul continues, Acts 15:41 tells us, "through Syria and Cilicia, strengthening the churches."

But when Christ is at the center of your friendship, it may change but it doesn't end. Cue Michael W. Smith here, singing "Friends are friends forever, if the Lord's the Lord of them."

It wasn't really over for Paul and Barnabas either. Even though they never saw each other again, and the last we do see of them together is them splitting up, we have some great clues that the gospel was greater than their disagreements. For instance, in 1 Corinthians 9:6, Paul mentions Barnabas after their "breakup," as if they are partners in spirit still!

Even better, Paul later says something about John Mark. Remember, he's the punk kid Paul didn't want on his journey and who really was the point of contention between Paul and Barnabas. In a letter to his young protégé Timothy, Paul says, "Bring Mark with you, for he is useful to me in the ministry" (2 Tim. 4:11).

How could Paul do this? How could his friendship be maintained after such conflict?

Well, his ultimate worth was not found in his friendships per se but in Jesus Christ. He knew that no friend could do for him what only God could do for him, which is why he was able to forgive and love people.

And this is true for you and me too. So long as we expect from people—our significant other, our kids, our parents, our roommates, our friends—something that only Jesus Christ can give us, we make an idol of them and an endlessly unsatisfied person of ourselves.

Human friendship cannot replace friendship with God. It simply wasn't made to. Christian friendship was meant to point to friendship with God, to glorify friendship with God, to remind us of friendship with God, but it cannot replace friendship with God.

Because even the best of friends cannot bear and endure *everything*. Not like God.

Some of you struggle with friendships. Be honest with yourself: Is it possible that one of the problems you have in making friends is that you place unreasonable expectations on them? That you are not satisfied with Jesus and his gospel, and so you bring this dissatisfaction into a relationship and expect from someone a meeting of needs that only Jesus can bring?

I have to tell you, he will bring it! He is the true friend who sticks closer than a brother.

In the Psalms, when David is lamenting time after time that all his friends have deserted him, he is crying out to the only sustenance he has, with friends or without: the God of the universe, who loves him and accepts him as he is. Only God can meet the deepest needs of your heart. Only God can quiet that ache. Only God can fulfill your soul. Only God can give you the peace that passes understanding.

And he does this through Jesus Christ, who, Luke 7:34 says, "is a friend of . . . sinners."

There's no better friend than God. If he is for you, who can be against you? And when you repent of your sins and put your trust in Jesus Christ alone for forgiveness and eternal life, you get him not just as your Master and Lord and Teacher but as your Friend.

Jesus says to his disciples, "I do not call you servants anymore, because a servant doesn't know what his master is doing. I have called you friends" (John 15:15). What a miracle!

We can bear all things, believe all things, hope all things, endure all things, because Christ has done that for us, and he gives us the power to do it for others.

When Love Comes to Town

Love never ends.

1 Corinthians 13:8

God's *hesedh* will never cease.

Leon Morris[1]

During all that "going around" with all those different girls I did in my youth, I was searching for something that kept eluding me. It was love, sure. But it was a certain kind of love. That *agape* love, I guess, that *hesedh* love. As a kid, I could not have understood that intellectually, but I certainly understood it emotionally.

I remember during my high school years especially, lying in bed at night, staring at the ceiling and wondering if I would ever really know love. Whether I had a girlfriend or not at the time—it almost didn't matter. The ache never went away. I think singer John Mayer gets very close to capturing that angst with these lyrics: "I can feel the love I want, I can feel the love I need, but it's never gonna come the way I am."[2]

He goes on to wonder if he'll ever see a change, the final end of that frustrating search for love, or if "it's always in the blood." Years before Mayer wrote these lyrics, night after night, I wondered the same thing. I bet you have too. Have you ever wondered if you will ever feel loved?

The Enemy did an incredible job of using those feelings against me. When I faced the dissatisfaction of earthly loves, when my self-interested romances never quite seemed to pan out, he would play on my fears and target my insecurities. He deftly moved from "Nobody loves you" to "Nobody *could* love you." Is it any wonder that my misadventures in romance were directly connected to a lack of assurance of my salvation?

I was trying to avoid accepting back then what I'm perfectly fine acknowledging today: I am not a naturally lovely person. I'm a mess, in fact. But I'm more sure today not just of my lack of loveliness but of Christ's loveliness for me.

In the Mood for Love

I don't know if you've ever thought about this, but I have: Did the disciples know they were loved? Like, in the middle of everything, throughout the Gospels, do they realize that what Jesus is doing for them is in fact loving?

So I checked. And I discovered that Jesus never says to his followers in any of the four Gospels any variation of the phrase "I love you"—*until* John 13:34. Almost to the end of the fourth Gospel, toward the end of the chapter, Jesus implicitly says "I love you" when he says, "Love one another. Just as I have loved you."

That's the first time he verbally references his love for his disciples. Oh sure, he talks a lot about people loving God and people loving each other, and in John 3 he talks about God loving the world, but Jesus never directly says, "Hey guys: I love you." In the middle of the rebukes, the dangers, the confusion, he never is like, "Peter, I know I called you the devil that time, but you know I love you, right?"

You don't think Peter was lying awake in bed that night, staring at the ceiling? Eyes wide, face pale, rehearsing the highlight of the day. "He called me Satan." You don't think Peter wondered if he was loved?

Do you ever wonder?

Do you ever lie awake at night under the weight of everything going on in your life or the weight of all the wounds that have accumulated throughout your life and think to yourself, *Is God . . . mad at me? Does he even love me?*

You may in fact believe God loves you, mainly because you grew up hearing it, but I'm convinced that most Christians haven't really scratched the surface of seeing how expansive God's love really is. They have settled for a sweet little sentimental religious understanding of God's love and have never contemplated it as forged in the blazing fires of his holiness.

So, just how loved are you?

At the beginning of John 13, we get a glimpse. It's not Jesus speaking but the Holy Spirit inspiring John: "Before the Passover Festival, Jesus knew that his hour had come to depart from this world to the Father. Having loved his own who were in the world, he loved them to the end" (v. 1).

What's fascinating is that this passage marks a turning point in the entire book. John 13:1 marks the introduction to the rest of John's Gospel. It is like Jesus's focus has changed. Narratively, he is not occupied so much with the public ministry of teaching and preaching as he is with tending to his friends and preparing for his death. "He knew that his hour had come to depart from the world." The urgency of the task has now come to bear.

He's gathered with his closest followers for this Passover meal. The shadow of the cross is looming larger over these thirteen men, and the time has come to drive home some eternally important points. And Jesus does this not by setting up a lectern or firing up the PowerPoint but by rolling up his sleeves and getting down on his hands and knees to wash his disciples' dirty feet.

Now, you and I know that can be a pretty gross thing to do. Once upon a time, when I was a pastor, I had the bonehead idea of preaching while I wandered the congregation, washing people's feet. The big idea, as I planned to preach an overview of the plan of redemption through the whole Bible, was to declare the God who "comes near," even as a man to serve. Sounds cool, right? I mean, I thought so. But even as I worked hard on the concept, I made a few crucial errors.

First, I'd spent years preaching from notes and manuscripts for a reason. Secondly, I'm a terrible multitasker. So trying to wash feet while recounting episodes from the Old Testament entirely from memory was a disaster.

Also, while I *did have* the forethought of prearranging with certain people permission to wash their feet that Sunday, I *hadn't* thought that everybody else wouldn't know that. Thus, as I made my way around the sanctuary with my little bowl and towel, trying to wax gospelicious on the patriarchs and the prophets, there was a palpable sense of panic in the room that I might choose just anybody's gnarly feet at random to unsheathe for the whole dadgummed congregation.

I don't know that anybody heard a single word I said. And that's just as well, since I don't know that my words were especially great that morning. I really hoped they heard the gospel through the gross-out.

But what Jesus was doing with his disciples is beyond gross-out. To get to the scandal of it, you have to understand that washing someone's feet at that time and culture was seen as the most menial, dishonorable task there could be. Some Jewish theologians at this time even argued that Jewish slaves shouldn't be required to wash feet, only gentile slaves. It was considered an act lower than low. And the only time someone would wash the feet of a peer, like a friend, perhaps, or a family member, would be in a rare act of special love. But there are no examples—zero—in either Jewish or Greco-Roman sources of the time of a superior washing the feet of an inferior. Except for John 13.

The God of the universe got down on his hands and knees to do the job even Jewish slaves were too good for.

Do you think you're loved? How loved do you think you are?

John 13:1, in fact, is where we see the fullness of Christ's love for his disciples both then and now.

We Were Born to Be Loved

The passage begins, "Having loved his own" (13:1). "Having loved," it says. In English verb tenses, this is a perfect progressive form. This means that it is a past action that is continuing in the present. So this tells us, first of all, that all Jesus has done has been done out of love. He didn't decide at this meal, "Hey, you know what? I *do* love you guys!"

No, he had been loving them all along. And he's been loving you all along.

When did he start?

Before time began. He was loving you before there was a you to love.

You know, I think one of the best practices many Christians could adopt is reading Romans 8 on a regular basis. Maybe every day. I think it's the greatest chapter in the Bible, or at least in the top five for sure. If you ever find yourself feeling a little lost or confused, maybe a little hopeless, like the hurts are just too heavy, or you're crushed by the weight of conviction of sin or just the pain of life, read Romans 8. Again and again and again.

And in Romans 8:29, we read something fascinating. It just blows my mind. "For those he foreknew he also predestined to be conformed to the image of his Son." Notice that it doesn't say, "For *what* he foreknew." It's not as if God looked through time, saw you'd be a good apple out of the rotten bushel, and picked you. It says, "For *those* he foreknew." It's a relational foreknowledge. Meaning, he knew you before there was a you, and he predestined you to be like Jesus.

Knowing everything, Christ loved you.

Do you ever think about that? Knowing *everything*, Christ loved you.

Most romance stories and love songs don't usually get this right. Love in these is always predicated on how one person makes the other feel. It's rare to find a depiction of love in our culture that resembles the kind of preemptive, "having loved" kind of love. But one movie that gets kind of close is Michel Gondry's *Eternal Sunshine of the Spotless Mind.*[3]

The film begins as many romantic comedies do, with a kind of "meet cute" between our two main characters. Joel (played by Jim Carrey) and Clementine (played by Kate Winslet) see each other and, of course, fall in love. What ensues gets weirder and weirder, however.

Joel and Clementine go on dates, take long walks on the beach, and spend lots of time together. But as in most romantic relationships, they are frequently beset by the challenges of their personalities and the conflicts of self-interest. What begins as a love story devolves. They go from loving each other to outright *hating* each other.

And here is where the movie gets *extra* weird. In the universe where *Eternal Sunshine* is set, it just so happens that there's a scientific firm called Lacuna that can erase select memories from willing minds. The two former lovebirds hate each other so much, they both undergo the process to remove any memory of the other from their brains. That's how strong their hatred has grown—they wish the other person didn't even exist.

But something occurs along the way. These two new "strangers" are thrust back together again. And what do you think happens?

Well, of course, love begins to take over again, though the employees of Lacuna try to stop it. In the end, Joel and Clementine discover that the procedure of memory erasure includes recording all the old memories. And these two are able to access that recording and see all the things they wanted to forget. Listening to these erased memories, pains and hurts and hatreds regurgitated, they now realize they knew each other before and the pain was too great to go on.

So what do you think they do?

They decide, despite it all, despite now knowing "ahead of time" how awful they once thought the other, to give it another go. Knowing everything, love is worth it.

There's kind of a biblical precedent for this sort of love. Think of the prophet Hosea. "When the LORD first spoke to Hosea, he said this to him: Go and marry a woman of promiscuity" (Hosea 1:2). Hosea was ordered to marry a prostitute.

Why would God command Hosea to do such a thing? He is creating through the prophet a real-world illustration of his own commitment to Israel. And as you keep reading in Hosea, you see God rebuking the spiritual adultery of his people. They've gone after other gods. They make repeated commitments to disobedience. They don't commit wholeheartedly to the one true God, YHWH. God has covenanted with them, but they are, every single day, cheating on him.

And this is in turn a picture of Christ and his bride, the church. He declares us righteous, spotless, clothed in his perfection, but doing so is an immense outpouring of grace, because every day, you and I decide, in some ways little and in some ways big, to cheat on Jesus with some other thing we think will satisfy us or justify us or give us peace. Every day we drift into decisions of the flesh and fail to give him all that he's due. Yet he never leaves! He has committed himself *from the beginning* to a people he knows will cheat on him.

Would you do that? Would any one of us, standing at the altar with our spouse-to-be, and, being able to see right into the future and know for certain . . .

In four years, your spouse is going to give up and stop paying you any attention.

In five years, your spouse is going to have an affair.

In six years, your spouse is going to become engaged in pornography and turn cold to you for a long time.

In ten years, your spouse is going to cheat on you with your best friend.

. . . would you still say "I do"?

These kinds of things happen to so many of us. Nobody gets married expecting to get divorced. We get married to the person we marry because we assume we've found the person who will never hurt us that way, never betray us. And yet the divorce rate continues to hover at 50 percent.

But we don't think *our* spouse would ever do such things. Which is precisely why we say cheerfully in the ceremonial moment, "I do."

Jesus sees everything. He stands at the altar with us, sees right through our veil, right through our fig leaves. He sees it all. Every doubt, every mistake, every sin, every choice made over a lifetime in which we say, "You don't satisfy, God; *this* will satisfy me right now." And yet when he's asked, "Do you take this sinner to be yours?" Jesus says resolutely, lovingly: "I do."

The "having loved" in John 13:1 is the commitment Christ makes from the beginning that he will never leave you nor forsake you—that there's nothing, in fact, you can do to get rid of him. "Having loved" you, he's going to keep loving you.

The kind of love Christ has for his bride is the kind of love that has seen it all and isn't going anywhere. You are loved from the very beginning.

Livin' on Love

But John 13:1 continues, "Having loved his own *who were in the world.*"

Do you know that God is not waiting for a better version of you to appear?

There's good news! Jesus loves the *real* you, not the pretend you that you want everybody to think you are. He isn't fooled; he isn't fazed. Whoever you are, whatever you're doing, wherever you've found yourself or chosen to go, nothing can separate you from his love.

"He loved his own who were in the world." What on earth can this mean? Why this emphasis? I think "in the world" in this instance means that, right in the thick of the disciples' confusion and their doubts and their sins, Jesus was loving them. He wasn't holding out on them.

The love of Christ is not a probationary love. He is not presenting you with some kind of contract, like, "Okay, if you will just clean up areas x, y, and z in your life, then you can have some of my love." No, he gives himself fully and freely to the real you.

That real you, the you inside whom you hide, the you whom you try to protect, the you whom you hope nobody sees or knows—*that's* the you whom God loves.

No, he doesn't love your sin, of course. He loves your true self. Without pretense, without façade, without image management, without the religious makeup. You the sinner, you the idolater, you the worshiper of false gods—*that's the you Jesus loves*.

This is the whole point of the Christian message: God loves sinners. Jesus died for sinners. He didn't wait for us to get our act together. He knew we never could! "While we were still helpless, at the right time, Christ died for the ungodly" (Rom. 5:6).

Tim Keller says, "The gospel is this: We are more sinful and flawed in ourselves than we ever dared believe, yet at the very same time we are more loved and accepted in Jesus Christ than we ever dared hope."[4]

If this is true, by the way, we can finally be our true selves.

I think this is what Martin Luther was getting at when he said to a friend in a letter, "Let your sins be strong" (often translated "sin boldly").[5] Did you ever hear that he said that? It can be confusing. Was Luther telling his friend to go on sinning like Paul says *not* to do in Romans 6:1–2? I don't think so. I think Luther meant that, because the good news is true, we can admit boldly that we are sinners!

And here's where a warning comes in with this way of understanding the true gospel: to say that Christ loves you right now, just as you are, is not to say that his love shouldn't or doesn't change you. It doesn't mean that he intends for you to stay exactly as you are. You can't clean yourself up for Jesus, but knowing the love of Jesus does have a cleansing effect! "Therefore, if anyone is in Christ, he is a new creation; the old has passed away, and see, the new has come" (2 Cor. 5:17).

To know this whole love, you must present your whole self, your whole sin, to him.

Here in John 13, Jesus comes to wash Peter's feet:

> "Lord, are you going to wash my feet?" [Peter asked.]
> Jesus answered him, "What I'm doing you don't realize now, but afterward you will understand."
> "You will never wash my feet," Peter said. (vv. 6–8)

Peter *seems* humble. But there is some self-righteousness there. Because to submit to washing means acknowledging we aren't clean.

> Jesus replied, "If I don't wash you, you have no part with me."
> Simon Peter said to him, "Lord, not only my feet, but also my hands and my head." (vv. 8–9)

The love of Jesus isn't something to dabble in. The atoning work of Christ isn't something you can have a little bit of. Please never think of Christianity as something you can just get your feet wet in.

> "One who has bathed," Jesus told him, "doesn't need to wash anything except his feet, but he is completely clean. You are clean, but not all of you." For he knew who would betray him. This is why he said, "Not all of you are clean." (vv. 10–11)

Jesus is talking about Judas, of course. And what's chilling about this scene is that Judas is there at this table, at this scene of love. We can even assume that Jesus washes Judas's feet! But Judas isn't washed, not in the way that counts. He is committed to his own way and is only a hanger-on when it comes to the love of Jesus. He's interested in the benefits but not the cost.

The danger of this kind of dabbling is immense. It puts you in the crosshairs not of God's love but of his terrible vengeance. This is how John puts it: "The one who believes in the Son has eternal life, but the one who rejects the Son will not see life; instead, the wrath of God remains on him" (3:36).

And here is Judas sitting at the table, getting his feet washed and no closer to salvation.

Is that you? Just going to church to get a little religion? Just trying to get a little bit of Jesus for your week? Are you willing to let Jesus wash your feet—get a little theology here and there, read a couple books, go to church, sing some songs, play along with the religious thing for a little while—but not put your whole body in? Are you refusing to give Jesus your whole self?

If you want his love, you can have it, but there's no halfway about it. He wants all of you. Many condemned people suffer from a little gospel. And you can have a little faith, but you cannot be saved by a little gospel, a halfway gospel, a "just get your feet wet" gospel.

Don't be like Judas. Don't just get your feet wet in God's grace; jump all the way in.

And to those willing to offer your broken self to Jesus, you will find his love waiting for you right now, this very moment. No delays, no hesitations, no reluctance. Right now, right here, whatever your circumstances, whatever your background, whatever your fears, whatever your doubts, whatever your hurts, whatever your sins, his love is for those who are in the world, for those who are in the thick of it. You can be in the sphere of his love right now.

To those who are suffering, he is sanctifying.

To those who are doubting, he is delivering.

For those who are hurting, he is comforting.

To those who are dying, he is holding.

For those who are sinning, he is advocating.

He will never let you go from his love.

You who are in the midst of this painful, broken world in a painful and broken life: he loves you. And while we are not perfect, his love *is*. And he will never stop.

You are loved from the beginning, and you are loved right now, right where you sit.

A Love without End, Amen

"Having loved his own who were in the world, *he loved them to the end*" (13:1, emphasis added).

The immediate referent here, of course, is to the cross. This is what John is referring to in verse 1 by "the hour for him to depart from the world." Jesus loved his own who were in the world so much, he was willing to go all the way to the end of the mission and die on the cross for their sins.

Look, if you think your sins aren't that big a deal, just take a look at the bloody cross where Jesus was killed for them. And where you see the wrath of God poured out for sins, see at the same time the great, immeasurable, vast, eternal love of God poured out for sinners.

Even the washing of feet that Jesus is doing in this moment is a picture of this. The phrase here translated in verse 4 as "he laid aside" (in reference to his outer garment) is the same translated elsewhere in the context of "laying down his life."

How loved are you? You are loved all the way to the cross.

Four chapters later, in what is called Jesus's High Priestly Prayer (John 17), while slumped down in spiritual anguish in the garden of Gethsemane, the cross looming ever closer now, Jesus is sweating blood—and he's thinking of you. He's carrying *your* sin. He's buckling under the weight of *your* disobedience. And John says that Jesus prays for himself, he prays for his disciples, and then he prays for all believers.

And I want to believe that in the space-time economy of the omnipresent-incarnate mind of our Lord, every name, face, and history of every believer who would ever live flashed through his mind. And in that garden, as he's preparing to take your sin to the cross to finally do away with it forever as far as God's judgment is concerned, he is praying for you *by name*.

"I am in them," Jesus says to the Father, "and you are in me, so that they may be made completely one, that the world may know you have sent me and have loved them as you have loved me" (17:23).

And then Jesus takes you to the cross with him. "Jesus didn't purchase 'save-ability,'" Paul Tripp says. "He took names to the cross!"[6]

He loves you to the end of his life.

But of course, he doesn't stay dead. He rises again. And while your sin stays in the grave, his love for you doesn't. It reigns and rules because *he* reigns and rules. Because of Christ's resurrection and ascension to the right hand of the Father, you are loved from the beginning all the way to the end, for all eternity.

He loves you completely. You are loved from the beginning. You are loved now. And you are loved forever.

Do you know what echoes in eternity? Not your stuff. Not your good intentions. Not your aspirations or your ambitions. Not even your romances. It is love. It is God's love.

This is the one thing that cannot be taken from you.

Paul writes, "Love never ends" (1 Cor. 13:8). And then a bit later, "Now these three remain: faith, hope, and love—but the greatest of these is love" (v. 13).

Love is carrying a lot of weight in these statements. And our flimsy notions of love—our sentimental love, our self-centered love—can't support what we see here. This love Paul is talking about is love with deep roots in the ground of God's steadfastness. Love is the greatest when it is grounded in the gospel.

Now, Jesus knows our capacity for love and forgiveness is finite. So how can he call us to persevere in these things toward others? The short answer, I think, is because God himself *perseveres in them toward us.* His eternal love fuels us.

After that time Jesus told Peter to forgive someone "seventy times seven" (Matt. 18:22), he went on to tell Peter a story about a servant who was forgiven a huge debt by his master. The servant, however, then goes on to punish a third party who owes the servant much less. When the master finds out, he has the debt-pardoned servant thrown in jail and tortured. Jesus then says—and this is the scary part—that's what will happen to us if, spurning the grace given us by God, we withhold grace from others (v. 35).

Because God's love toward us is relentlessly patient in its eternal perseverance, we have no Christian right to say to someone who has wronged us, even if they continue to wrong us, "You have reached your limit with me. My love for you stops now." Doing so fails to truly see the depths of our sin in the light of God's holiness. And if God, who is perfect and holy, will forgive and love we who are most certainly not, what basis do we have to be unforgiving and unloving to others?

And when we realize how much we've been forgiven, the verse "Love never ends" makes much more sense.

We need faith in God to see the logic of this. And the sure hope that he will sort it out. Faith and hope will take us all the way to the day love conquers all and everything sad becomes untrue.

See, faith isn't needed in the new heaven and new earth, because if faith is the conviction of things not seen, we won't need it once we've "seen" (1 Cor. 13:12). And our hope will be fulfilled then too, because we will finally have Christ, our hope of glory. So we won't need faith and hope in heaven. We need them to *get there*, of course, but not after.

But love? We will keep loving forever because we will be loved forever. Love will never end.

"Having loved his own who were in the world, he loved them to the end" (John 13:1).

Now That We've Found Love

When the perfect comes, the partial will come to an end. . . . For now we see only a reflection as in a mirror, but then face to face.

1 Corinthians 13:10, 12

Our unworthiness makes God's love all the more lovely.

Matthew Barrett[1]

I am firmly ensconced in middle age, which brings with it the regular, demoralizing signs of getting old. One of the more surprising signs of getting older is my sudden interest in country music. Now, I've always been one who likes many kinds of music. My tastes genuinely are eclectic. But when anybody asked me when I was younger, "What kind of music do you like?" I would answer, "Anything but country." I'd listen to pop, metal, classical, hip-hop, you name it. But not country.

And this is how I know I'm getting old. One day, the radio in my car was somehow inexplicably tuned to the country station, and I just left it there. (You can also tell I'm old by the fact that I still listen to the car radio.)

My teenage daughters, of course, are just like me when I was younger. They like everything *but country*. So, as a good dad, I'll leave it on and often turn it up. I'm "that dad" who, when I'm dropping them off for school, cranks up the volume as they open the door to join their friends. Nothing like making a super cool entrance to the tune of "Boot Scootin' Boogie."

I don't know why I've left my tuner on the country station for so long. I just started liking it, I guess. But I will readily acknowledge that most of the newer country songs are utter rubbish. A lot of them seem to revolve around the same idea: driving a truck down to a body of water, wherein a girl eventually ends up dancing in the back. This has literally never happened in the history of life, but apparently we need forty-eight country songs about it.

But every now and then, there's a gem. Something thoughtful breaks through. May I present to you the only new country song that's made me cry? It's called "If I Told You," and it's sung by Darius Rucker. Now, here's how else you know I'm old: I remember when Darius Rucker was named Hootie. But now he's Darius, and he's singing a song about a love that sounds suspiciously like grace, with lyrics like: "If I told you the mess that I can be when there's no one there to see, could you look the other way? Could you love me anyway?"[2]

You should look it up online and read all the lyrics. It's actually pretty deep, isn't it?

I'm convinced this is the most significant yearning of our hearts. Beneath all other desires and longings, the deepest desire and longing we each have, no matter how we express it, is to be totally known and at the same time totally loved. "Could you love me anyway?" We all want to be loved, but really, we all want to be loved *anyway*.

Paul writes,

> For we know in part, and we prophesy in part, but when the perfect comes, the partial will come to an end. When I was a child, I spoke like a child, I thought like a child, I reasoned like a child. When I became a man, I put aside childish things. For now we see only a reflection as in a mirror, but then face to face. Now I know in part, but then I will know fully, as I am fully known. (1 Cor. 13:9–12)

Something must prepare us well for the day we will see Jesus face-to-face and know him as he knows us. Because while he is invisible now, we nevertheless struggle to face him. We run from him in our prayers. We turn away from him in our sins. The idea of coming face-to-face with God, whether in spirit or in the flesh, is far too intimidating, too *dangerous* even. We are utterly unworthy. Which is why we hide.

And it's the fear that the "love me anyway" kind of love isn't real, isn't true, and cannot be ours that prompts us to put up walls and protective layers, façades to manage our images. We desperately want to believe we can be "loved anyway," but we secretly fear such a love isn't possible.

Well, it's this kind of love that the apostle John dares us to believe in and outright declares is ours for the having in his first letter. And this is why he speaks rather strongly about coming out from hiding.

This is the message we have heard from him and declare to you: God is light, and there is absolutely no darkness in him. If we say, "We have fellowship with him," and yet we walk in darkness, we are lying and are not practicing the truth. If we walk in the light as he himself is in the light, we have fellowship with one another, and the blood of Jesus his Son cleanses us from all sin. (1 John 1:5–7)

You've Got to Hide Your Love Away

A couple of years ago, I was on an airplane coming in for a landing when something went very wrong. We had just descended below some thick clouds. The landing gear was already down. I could see buildings and lights below very close and getting closer. Suddenly, the plane lurched back upward. Its whole body shook violently, and it felt like we were heading straight up into the sky.

The experience was jarring, scary. People began pulling out their earbuds and closing their books, looking around at each other. None of us knew what had happened. There was a palpable sense of fear in the cabin.

Eventually we leveled off, and as we circled in the sky, the pilot came on the intercom to helpfully apologize and share that there had been another plane on the runway, right where we were supposed to land.

This startled me for a couple of reasons. First, I had no idea to that point that the pilots were just eyeballing the whole landing thing. I always assumed there was some person in a tower who looked down and then radioed them to say, "Yep, all good, come on down." But apparently these folks are just dropping out of the sky and seeing at the last minute whether the runway's clear or not.

Second, I almost died. Now, I have a lot of "I almost died" stories, and my wife discounts them all, but I promise you this one is real. I'm not an aerospace engineer or a physics master, but I'm fairly certain that if one airplane crashes into another airplane, and if you happen to be on one of those airplanes, you will die. So yeah—I almost died.

Later, as I thought about this incident, replaying it over and over in my head, I reflected on what exactly I had done in the moment. And I realized that at the moment the plane lurched back into the sky, when I felt the whole thing was going to explode, I instinctively put my hand up over my face.

Why on earth did I do that?

I thought about it for a bit. I wondered if it was so nobody else could see that I was scared. I wondered if it was so I couldn't see anything scary about to happen. But it wasn't a thoughtful act at all. It was an impulse.

And the more I thought about it, the more I realized this impulse has been in me since infancy. It's always been in all of us. Think about it: when you were a child, and you got up in the middle of the night to go use the restroom or get a drink of water, you would tiptoe on the way there and run like lightning all the way back to bed. Why? So the boogeyman wouldn't get you, of course.

And when you hurled yourself desperately back into your bed, to save your life from the boogeyman obviously hot on your heels, what did you do?

That's right. You got under the covers. Your blanket was a perfect force field against the boogeyman. He was powerless against your cartoon-themed bedspread.

And this is just an impulse from the beginning of time.

Freshly into their disobedience, feeling the new and crushing weight of guilt, shame, and death, Adam and Eve realize their attempt at godhood has in a way made them somehow less than human. They don't feel powerful at all. They feel very vulnerable, very exposed, very scared. And what do they do?

They sew fig leaves together to make coverings for themselves. And then, when they hear the Lord coming, they hide in the bushes. And we've been trying to hide our sin and shame ever since.

But there's a problem with this. Because just as the Lord came looking for Adam and Eve, when we encounter the living God, there is no hope of hiding anything from him.

John says, "God is light, and there is absolutely no darkness in him" (1 John 1:5).

This is a parallelism, very similar to what we see in a lot of Hebrew poetry—in many of the Psalms, for instance. It is the same thought repeated but in a different way. First the positive version is given: "God is light." And then the same thought is repeated from the negative side: "and there is absolutely no darkness in him."

The point of this is the emphasis. *God is light.* Which means no darkness can abide in him. What happens to darkness when you turn the light on in a room? It disappears. It is vanquished.

And God is pure light. We see the kind of light God is throughout the pages of the Old Testament, where he leads the Israelites by fire and reveals his holy law on mountaintops with such blazing brightness that the face of its recipient glows thereafter. Even if you were to hide in the cleft of a rock, and only the backside of this glory came by you, you'd be lit up.

The light of God is pure and perfect. It illuminates and exposes. That's what light does. And that's what God does. In essence, what John is helping us to see is that the light of God reveals everything.

Sunshine of Your Love

The truth is, we cannot hide from God.

Oh, but we try, don't we?

I think of that Samaritan woman Jesus waits for at Jacob's well. She has clearly been looking for love all her life. She carries a burdensome shame. She is a sinner, yes, and also likely a victim of exploitation several times over.

We can deduce she is trying to be alone because she goes to draw water in the middle of the day. Most people would make this trek in the cool of the morning and the cool of the evening. She goes in the hottest part of the day, likely because she's tired of being looked at sideways, gossiped about, embarrassed, or accused.

As Jesus begins to speak to her, he does what he always does—he goes for the heart. But she deflects, trying to keep the conversation on the chitchat level. She doesn't want anyone invading her personal space. She ends up trying to stiff-arm Jesus.

Are you doing that? Maybe you're doing it with religion. Do you think if you just study enough theology and do enough Bible studies that you can keep Jesus out from the areas of your heart he really wants to get at? Isn't it weird how we do that? Are you trying to stiff-arm Jesus with your religiosity?

One thing we learn about the real Jesus is that he is not a great respecter of personal space. You may be able to keep your friends and family and everybody else at arm's length, only letting them see what you want them to see, but you can't do that with Jesus. He sees your heart, and he will go after it.

I think of Jesus with that rich young ruler. This guy wanted Jesus to accept everything he was *willing* to give. But Jesus knew what was in his heart. And so he asked for that.

In fact, I very often think that the areas of our lives we are most desperate to protect are the very areas Jesus most wants to deal with in us.

John says, "There is absolutely no darkness in him." To the extent you are dwelling in the dark is the extent to which you have not surrendered to the healing holiness of God.

Just think about it: hiding makes no sense! Consider these words from Psalm 139 (my paraphrase): "Where can I go to escape you? Nowhere! If I go up into the sky, you're there. If I dig a hole deep in the earth, you're there. You know every secret thing." And Jesus says in Mark 4:22, "For there is nothing hidden that will not be revealed, and nothing concealed that will not be brought to light."

"If we say, 'We have fellowship with him,' and yet we walk in darkness, we are lying and are not practicing the truth" (1 John 1:6). And because there is no darkness in God at all, I'd also suggest that if we say, "We walk in darkness," we are also lying, because while we might be able to conceal ourselves from everyone else, we can never conceal ourselves from God. There is no darkness so dark, no corner so hidden, no sin so secret that it is not seen by the God who is light.

We should not hide from God. And because he sees everything, knows everything, will eventually reveal everything, we *cannot* hide from God.

But there's a plot twist in this passage.

Bold as Love

There is a really curious connection John makes here. It is similar to what he does later in his letter when he refers to the love of God. "Dear friends," he writes, "let us love one another, because love is from God, and everyone who loves has been born of God and knows God. The one who does not love does not know God, because God is love" (4:7–8).

Notice he isn't simply saying that God is love and therefore you can be loved by God and give love to God. He is saying,

"God is love and therefore you should love others." And as in our text here, he states it negatively as well: "If you don't love others, you don't know God."

How does he use the same rhetoric in his talk of God's light in chapter 1? "If we say, 'We have fellowship with him,' and yet we walk in darkness, we are lying and are not practicing the truth" (v. 6). In other words, if you walk in darkness, you are not experiencing fellowship with God. But it's not just fellowship *with God* that the light of God impacts. Consider verse 7: "If we walk in the light as he himself is in the light, we have fellowship with one another."

Notice it doesn't say "we have fellowship with *him*." It is true that to walk in the light of God is to have fellowship with God—that's the point of verse 6—but John writes, "If we walk in the light . . . we have fellowship with *one another*" (emphasis added).

Why does he put it that way?

I think it's because if Christian brothers and sisters aren't honest and transparent and confessional with each other, we don't really have fellowship with each other's true selves, do we? We hide certain things from each other, mainly out of self-protection, out of fear, out of risk-avoidance and a sense of shame, and thus we end up not really knowing each other. We just know the best version of each other we manage to work up when it's time to play church.

John is shining the light of Christ into the religious charade so many call church.

Now, no one, least of all Christ Jesus, is suggesting that being real with each other poses no risk. It can cost us embarrassment. It can cost us reputation. It can cost us hurt. But the light will expose all of this eventually anyway. And the testimony of the New Testament, which doesn't know of a church community without sin and brokenness in it, is that the cost of hiding is much greater than the cost of being exposed.

Jesus's own brother James, in his epistle, even connects confession to healing (5:16). We cannot love each other if we don't actually know each other.

In my time as a pastor, I heard nearly everything confessed. And it happened so often that when people came in for counseling, and they hemmed and hawed, I knew they were working up to some kind of personal revelation. As a ministry leader, I represented God to many people. And the reason they beat around the bush in my presence was because they were afraid. I saw it as part of my job, as an undershepherd of Christ, to receive them as I imagined Christ would.

I remember one day when this particular lady, a dear friend of ours named Tonya, who came to saving faith in our church and who I had the privilege of baptizing, came to visit with me in my study. I could tell right off the bat she was very nervous. She was jittery, skittish. The chair she sat in was practically shaking on the floor.

We played the chitchat thing for a while. But eventually I decided to rescue her and break the ice. I said to her, "Tonya, is there a dead body in your trunk?"

She stopped cold. She looked at me with the biggest eyes. I could tell she was trying to process what I had said. Eventually, she sputtered, "Do I . . . what did you say?"

"I said," I reiterated, "is there a corpse in the trunk of your car?"

She reared back. "No," she said, clearly mortified I'd ask such a thing. "Why would you ask me that?"

"Because," I said, "I've heard all kinds of confessions in this room. I've heard all sorts of things. But I've never heard anybody say they had a dead body in their trunk. Now, if you do, we can figure out what to do about it together. But if you don't, you can just take a deep breath and tell me what you came to tell me."

She laughed slightly. Then she took a deep breath, and she told me about her secret shame. Years previous, she had committed adultery. This was before she was a believer, but she knew it was wrong then, and after a while she cut off the relationship and confessed it to her husband. She was sorry she had committed this sin, and she had worked hard to prove to her husband ever since that she would never do something like that again.

Tonya's husband, not a believer, said he forgave her. But this offense of hers became his winning hand in any argument. He kept her shame in his back pocket, ready to bring it out at any moment. She lived constantly in an environment of condemnation and shame, as he would never let her forget what she'd done to him.

I listened patiently as she, through tears, shared how lonely she felt, how unforgiven she felt, how scared she felt that this sin would always plague her, always be that scarlet letter on her chest. Of course, I could not do anything about the disposition of her husband. But I reminded her that Jesus's news for us is good, that he really has taken all of our sin to the cross with him and canceled it, forgave it, killed it there with his own death. I told her, with the authority of God's Word and the grace of God's gospel, that her sins were forgiven, and no matter what fallen person aimed to lord them over her, the holy Lord of all did not and never would.

In fact, if you bring up your old, repented-of sin to God, he effectively says to you, "What are you talking about?" He has forgotten it. To punish you with the memory of it now would be to suggest that his Son's death was not sufficient.

But I knew well why Tonya was afraid. I had felt that fear too. When I was in my period of secret shame and serious depression, I was still playing the church game. I was attending a men's community group at my church, and everybody there thought I was an awesome guy. I had no desire to bust their illusion! So I played along, kept up a cheerful face, lied about how things were at home, and never let anybody get a peek at the battle waging in my heart and mind. At some point in the life of our group, someone suggested we read Dietrich Bonhoeffer's *Life Together*. And I was completely discombobulated by the whole thing. I remember reading the following passage, in fact, and somehow, in some way, finally feeling *seen*.

> He who is alone with his sin is utterly alone. It may be that Christians, notwithstanding corporate worship, common prayer, and all their fellowship in service, may still be left to their loneliness. The final break-through to fellowship does not occur, because, though they have fellowship with one another as believers and as devout people, they do not have fellowship as the undevout, as sinners. The pious fellowship permits no one to be a sinner. . . . Many Christians are unthinkably horrified when a real sinner is suddenly discovered among the righteous. So we remain alone with our sin, living in lies and hypocrisy. . . .
>
> But it is the grace of the Gospel, which is so hard for the pious to understand, that it confronts us with the truth

and says: You are a sinner, a great, desperate sinner; now come, as the sinner that you are, to God who loves you. He wants you as you are; He does not want anything from you, a sacrifice, a work; He wants you alone. . . . You can hide nothing from God. The mask you wear before men will do you no good before Him. He wants to see you as you are, He wants to be gracious to you. You do not have to go on lying to yourself and your brothers . . . you can dare to be a sinner. Thank God for that; He loves the sinner but He hates sin.[3]

Look, I know the reasons we don't live transparently with each other. We're afraid. We're embarrassed. We don't want to be a burden. We don't want to be judged.

We also don't want to become someone's project! *If I tell people about this*, we think, *then they're going to feel like they have to look after me, and I'll become frustrating and draining to them.* This may sound humble, but it's prideful self-pity.

What all of this amounts to is a distrust in God himself. I know people are mean, I know people are judgmental, I know people act weird. But if I believe in the gospel, I do not have a choice any longer to live in the dark. "If we . . . walk in darkness, we are lying and are not practicing the truth" (1 John 1:6).

I must ask myself, *Do I want to get out of this experience on earth all that the gospel would empower me to get? Do I want to walk in the light around every corner? Do I let fear of judgment and worry about reputation rule my life?*

Jesus told a story in Matthew 25 about talents. A rich man had three servants. Before going on a long journey, he gave them each a measure of investment. When he returned, two guys had doubled their investment, but the only guy the master got mad at was the one who buried his talent in the ground, afraid of doing anything with it.

So I think, *Do I want to face my heavenly Father with sin still hidden?* "See? I kept it nice and secret. I stayed nice and safe. I fooled everyone."

Do I want to get to heaven having held out on you, my brothers and sisters? Do I expect to get to heaven and hear Jesus say, "Great job never opening up to anybody. You really maximized your time on earth."

I know that it's fear that keeps us from doing this, but this is what faith is given for. John is making a total connection between our fellowship with one another, our walking in the light, and our practicing the truth. It's a package deal. To believe the gospel is to turn from sin to Jesus, to turn from darkness to light, and to turn from solitude to fellowship.

You can affirm the gospel as true intellectually and yet live as if it's not true. This is the call John is making. If God is light and you walk in darkness, what does that say about your belief in the gospel?

Look, the whole point of church is so that no sinner seeking Jesus has to do it alone. And it doesn't matter what category of sin or struggle you have, the church of God has as much room as the grace of God will hold. The body of Christ has no overflow room.

What might God do with our churches if we simply opened up to him and to each other? We can dare to say, "Lord, do what you will, even if it's embarrassing to us, so long as it's honoring to you. Here's a blank check."

And here's the deal: when we take this risk, we can finally get to see how brilliant the light of the gospel really is. We'll get to see just how far grace goes.

We can stop hiding because of everything the gospel does, like freeing us from condemnation, counting us totally righteous in Jesus Christ, liberating us from a spirit of fear, and—glory be!—covering us eternally in his irrevocable love. You don't have to be afraid of shame and condemnation.

Loves Me Like a Rock

Why did Jesus expose the sin and shame of the woman at the well? To cover it. Why did Jesus puncture the rich young ruler's self-righteous religiosity? Because he wanted him to trade it in for the treasure of Christ himself.

The same light that exposes us heals us.

We get a picture of this in those early pages of the Bible, right after the fall. As Adam and Eve are called to account, do you remember what God does? They had covered themselves in fig leaves—just like we do. But he covers them instead with something else: "The LORD God made clothing from skins for the man and his wife, and he clothed them" (Gen. 3:21).

In a way, this is evidence of the first sacrifice. Adam and Eve had brought death into the world, and he's showing them that only death will cover them now. And this is perhaps the first foreshadow of Christ's sacrifice for us, the shedding of his blood that covers us from all unrighteousness. Which is exactly where John goes next: "If we walk in the light as he himself is in the light, we have fellowship with one another, *in our unworthiness makes God's love more startlingly beautiful.*

and the blood of Jesus his Son cleanses us from all sin"
(1 John 1:7).

We have to understand just how much this sacrifice has
purchased! His blood has delivered us from the domain of
darkness. His blood speaks the better word of justice accomplished. His blood declares pardon for us, cleansing for
us, and this cleansing pardon is an ongoing reality for the
believer. Christian, you are never *not* covered by the blood
of Jesus.

Here's another visit from ol' Kierkegaard:

> Love in him was pure action. There was no moment, not a
> single one in his life, when love in him was merely the inac-
> tivity of feeling. . . . His love was completely present in the
> least things as in the greatest; it did not gather its strength
> in single great moments as if the hours of everyday life were
> outside the requirements of the law. It was equally present
> in every moment, no greater when he breathed his last on
> the cross than when he suffered himself to be born. It was
> the same love which said, "Mary has chosen the good por-
> tion" and the same love which rebuked with a glance—or
> forgave—Peter. It was the same love when he received the
> disciples who joyfully returned home after performing mir-
> acles in his name and the same love when he found them
> sleeping.[4]

In other words, the blood of Christ, which covers us per-
petually, is a reminder that everything Christ does for us, to
us, in us, and through us is an act of pure love. He has always
loved us, is currently loving us, and will always love us.

If his blood has covered your sin, why are you still walking
in fear and hiding?

You know, the one place I finally felt "at home" I eventually got chewed up in and spit out of. I've had a pretty good life, but I've also got some pretty good reasons to keep entirely to myself and never let you or anyone else in. That would be the safest and, to some extent, the most understandable way for me to live my life.

And yet here comes my Savior, who ought not be embarrassed by anything. He has no sin. He needs no shame. And while I'm piling up as many fig leaves as I think it might take to impress you and distract you, Jesus is exposing himself to all the hurt, all the pain, all the weakness, all the condemnation that I am desperately trying to avoid. You cannot be any more exposed than Christ was on the cross. And he went there. For us.

And here is what else John means by "the light"—he means a vision of the glory of God, the radiance of his loveliness exemplified in his cross and resurrection and ascension. The illuminating vision that captivates sinners desperate for salvation. In the early verses of his Gospel, John writes,

> In him was life, and that life was the light of men. That light shines in the darkness, and yet the darkness did not overcome it. . . . The true light that gives light to everyone was coming into the world. (1:4–5, 9)

Shortly thereafter he records John the Baptist crying out, "Behold, the Lamb of God, who takes away the sin of the world!" (1:29 ESV). Or, as Isaiah 9:2 says, "The people walking in darkness have seen a great light."

You can't even see clearly when you're hiding! But when you're found? Suddenly you see.

Paul uses this same vision talk in Colossians 3:1, when he says, "If you have been raised with Christ, seek the things above, where Christ is, seated at the right hand of God." And then he says—in what's become one of my all-time favorite Bible verses—"For you died, and your life is hidden with Christ in God" (v. 3).

Oh, to be hidden with Christ in God! See, the gospel isn't trying to expose us to shame us. The good news is that Christ was exposed for us so that we can confess without fear and find our refuge in him. If we are hidden with Christ in God, we have nothing left to hide! It may cost us a little something, but the reward for walking in the light far surpasses keeping secret whatever it is we're trying to protect.

He is sure and steady. He is a rock of refuge. His love will anchor and comfort you all your days.

One of my favorite scenes from C. S. Lewis's Narnia stories comes from *The Voyage of the Dawn Treader*, where Eustace Scrubb—who is about as cuddly a personality as his name would suggest—finds himself in a scaly predicament. Eustace comes across a great treasure, and overcome with greed, he begins to imagine all the comforts of life he could enjoy with this treasure. He goes into "hoarding" mode. But eventually he falls asleep, and when he wakes up, he discovers he's become a dragon.

Why a dragon? Well, because dragons are hoarders. They protect their secret fortunes at all costs. And they also physically represent a kind of protection, don't they? They have heavy, scaly skin. They are covered in fleshy armor.

Eustace doesn't quite understand how he's gotten into this situation, but he becomes afraid. Before his nap, he'd put a gold bracelet around his wrist, and now that his arm has grown to dragon size, it is digging into him, constricting him, just like our secrets will do to us eventually. And he realizes that, as a dragon, he's been cut off from humanity, just like our hiding will do to us eventually.

And then Aslan the lion arrives on the scene. And Aslan leads Eustace to a garden where there's a well, and Eustace just knows if he can get into the water in the well, he will be healed. But he can't get in the way he is.

Aslan tells Eustace the dragon-boy that he will need to be undressed. Eustace, of course, recoils at the idea, pondering the lion's razor-sharp claws. But his desperation wins out.

He lays himself flat on the ground, and Aslan begins to tear his scaly armor away.

"When he began pulling the skin off," Eustace says, "it hurt worse than anything I've ever felt. The only thing that made me able to bear it was just the pleasure of feeling the stuff peel off."[5]

Eventually all of Eustace's gnarly dragon-skin, thick and rough, is laying on the grass beside him. And then Aslan does something else. He scoops up the freshly peeled dragon-boy and throws him into the water. And it stings something vicious! "But," Eustace said, "only for a moment. After that it became perfectly delicious."[6] He begins to frolic in the water and swim around. And then he discovers the pain in his arm is gone too. He realizes why. He's been transformed back into a real boy.

Look, walking in the light may sting a little. Heck, it may sting a lot. But it is far preferable to life in the dark. And on top of that, it is the only way to healing.

If we walk in the light, his blood cleanses us. You know, Jesus only deals with us on the playing field of reality. So come to him *as a sinner*. You cannot hide from God's gospel anyway. Come as a real person to the family God's gospel has made. We must not hide from each other. Come and be cleansed by his blood and hidden forever in the safety of Christ himself.

When Love Comes to Life

The glory of God's love has come to us in Christ, and it is coming again in Christ at his return. We don't have to be afraid. We don't have to hide. Hidden with Christ in God, we can look to heaven as our blessed hope, the day when all our fears and sins are ultimately vanquished and all we know is love. There is a reason Paul concludes his love chapter with a vision of heaven.

> For now we see only a reflection as in a mirror, but then face to face. Now I know in part, but then I will know fully, as I am fully known. Now these three remain: faith, hope, and love—but the greatest of these is love. (1 Cor. 13:12–13)

The love we experience now in our faulty, failing ways, in our fear and in our flesh, is just a pale reflection of what is to come. That day we will know as we are known, love as we are loved. It will be beyond the utmost bliss we can imagine.

And we have a taste of it even now, though pale. We find it in the true gospel, which announces love for sinners is real and available to anyone who wants it. Jesus indeed "loves us anyway." And in heaven, there will be no "anyway" anymore. There will be no sin to overlook, no brokenness to tolerate, no grief or suffering or anxiety.

Heaven will finish swallowing us up, and we will finally know the love we believe in blindly now. Love will be all there is. "In every heart in heaven," Jonathan Edwards says, "love dwells and reigns."[7]

Love has come. Love is here. And love is coming.

Be still our beating hearts.

Conclusion

Were The Beatles right that all we need is love?

Well, yes, but not in the way they understood love. Their love was ethereal and conditional, all flitter and feelings. The band broke up. Paul McCartney kept on writing "silly love songs" while John Lennon compared himself to Jesus in his love song to Yoko Ono. They are proof that sometimes geniuses have no idea what they're talking about.

I love The Beatles, but give me Hootie on this one. Give me "love me anyway." That's the kind of love that knows what it's looking at, sees what's been hidden, and doesn't walk away.

D. A. Carson contrasts the two major ways we conceive of God's love like this:

> So now God comes to us and says, "I love you." What does he mean?
>
> Does he mean something like this? "You mean everything to me. I can't live without you. Your personality, your witty conversation, your beauty, your smile—everything about you

transfixes me. Heaven would be boring without you. I love you!" That, after all, is pretty close to what some therapeutic approaches to the love of God spell out. We must be pretty wonderful because God loves us. And dear old God is pretty vulnerable, finding himself in a dreadful state unless we say yes. . . .

When he says he loves us, does not God rather mean something like the following? "Morally speaking, you are the people of the halitosis, the bulbous nose, the greasy hair, the disjointed knees, the abominable personality. Your sins have made you disgustingly ugly. But *I love you anyway*, not because you are attractive but because it is my nature to love."[1]

See, this is good news. Our states are constantly changing. We are not always lovable. We are not always attractive. Most of us are frequently neither lovable nor attractive! But God is unchanging. So the kind of love we need, the kind we really want, is the kind that God actually has for us. It's the kind God actually *is*—for us.

God is the one who sees with total clarity and knowledge the mess that we can be. And he loves us anyway.

It is true that all we need is love, but only because perfect love that perfects *us* can only be found in the God who is love in himself. All you need is love, because if you have the God who is love, you have all you truly need.

That we feel this love imperfectly for the moment does not mean the love isn't perfect. It means *we* aren't. But, strangely enough, it's through our imperfections, through our failures to feel loved and to give love, that having and sharing the love of God can actually tell us even more about God and the love that he is.

Jesus is patient and kind; he is not envious or boastful; he's not arrogant or rude. He did not insist on his own way but, following his Father's will, left the glory of heaven to empty himself and serve us and sacrifice himself for us.

Jesus isn't irritable or resentful. Jesus keeps no record of wrongs that he might rejoice over us in our sins and failings—for he has forgiven us all our trespasses, throwing our sins into the depths of the sea to remember them no more, and has justified us. Jesus rejoices with the truth of his grace that declares us righteous. So that in Jesus we can bear all things, believe all things, hope all things, endure all things.

Jesus never ends.

His loving-kindness endures forever. His loving-kindness is better than your next breath. And at your last breath, when all else fails, when all you can't take with you must be left behind, his love will carry you even deeper into his love. When you have no more need for food, no more need for water, no more need for shelter, his love will still be all of that for you—and more.

Because the one thing you can't live without isn't a thing at all. All that you will have left is the One who is the end-all, be-all, in and of himself. And if you have God, you have everything you need. The One who is love will be the only true thing you can count on when all is said and done. Indeed, he is the only true thing you can count on right this very moment.

And if you want a love song, consider the one he is singing over you:

> The LORD your God is among you,
> a warrior who saves.

He will rejoice over you with gladness.
He will be quiet in his love.
He will delight in you with singing. (Zeph. 3:17)

And look forward to the one we will be singing forever over him:

Worthy is the Lamb who was slaughtered
to receive power and riches
and wisdom and strength
and honor and glory and blessing! . . .
Blessing and honor and glory and power
be to the one seated on the throne,
and to the Lamb, forever and ever! (Rev. 5:12–13)

Acknowledgments

Writing a book about love is like playing with LEGOs in front of the Taj Mahal. It is impossible not to feel puny and inadequate. This project has been an exercise in engaging with ideas too weighty for me, far greater and much deeper than I can comprehend. But I have had a lot of help.

I first should apologize to every songwriter, singer, and band whose songs I shamelessly co-opted for chapter titles and subheadings, especially The Beatles and U2. But I could not have sustained the energy needed to endure in this work without songs like theirs. The soundtrack for this project was also amply supplied by Bob Dylan and Sirius XM's "oldies" station, 50s on 5.

You will also notice I leaned heavily on heavier thinkers like C. S. Lewis and Søren Kierkegaard and a good deal of others besides. I did double duty in preparing for this book and completing a project for my doctoral studies by reading a bunch of big books on love. Nothing helpful in these pages is original to me.

I suppose I should nod as well to all the exes I left in Texas. I spared us all the embarrassment by changing nearly everybody's names. I even moved out of Tennessee, just to be safe.

This book could not have been written without the support of the leaders, faculty, and students of Spurgeon College and Midwestern Seminary, where I am blessed to serve as Author in Residence. Thank you all for the constant encouragement and the expectation to write.

I wrote this book while my pastor Nathan Rose was working on his own doctoral dissertation, and we commiserated together on many Thursdays about how far behind we each were. I was glad to have a partner in procrastination. (I do think I finished first, though, so I win.)

This was a difficult book to write for lots of reasons, some of which may be obvious from the preceding pages. Therefore, I am thankful for my editor Brian Thomasson, who demonstrated a gracious patience and certainly a hoping and bearing of all things, especially while liking and commenting on my social media updates when he knew I should have been working.

All the good folks at Baker Books are too sweet for giving me the opportunity to revel in the gospel for them yet again.

Thank you, reader, for reading (even pages like the Acknowledgments that most people skip).

The three ladies I love most are the ones who love me most. Becky, Macy, and Grace—you are daily reminders of God's faithfulness to me. Thanks for tolerating my weirdness and even enjoying it from time to time. I will never be worthy of you. I swoon.

And finally, I am thankful for Jesus, who loves me without shame and without pretense and without holding anything against me. To be friends with the Lord of all is astounding to me. I stagger.

Notes

Introduction

1. C. S. Lewis, *Perelandra* (New York: Macmillan, 1965), 201.

2. Larry Norman, "Reader's Digest," *Only Visiting This Planet* (Verve, 1972).

3. C. S. Lewis, *Mere Christianity* (Westwood, NJ: Barbour, 1952), 115.

Chapter 1 What's Love Got to Do with It?

1. Peter Kreeft, *The God Who Loves You: Knowing the Height, Depth, and Breadth of God's Love for You* (Ann Arbor, MI: Servant, 1988), 146.

2. *The Wonder Years* (New World Television, The Black/Marlens Company: 1988–93, ABC).

3. Bruce Marshall, *The World, the Flesh and Father Smith* (Boston: Houghton Mifflin, 1945), 108.

4. Paul David Tripp, *What Did You Expect?: Redeeming the Realities of Marriage* (Wheaton: Crossway, 2010), 56–57.

5. Katherine Harmon, "How Important Is Contact with Your Infant?," *Scientific American*, May 6, 2010, https://www.scientificamerican.com /article/infant-touch/.

6. You can watch Mez give a shortened version of his testimony here: "Mez McConnell—Loved by the Ones He Mocked," YouTube video, 3:36, uploaded by Together for the Gospel (T4G), June 20, 2016, https:// www.youtube.com/watch?v=18iViUKMmNc.

Chapter 2 Will You Still Love Me Tomorrow?

1. St. John Chrysostom, *The Love Chapter: The Meaning of First Corinthians* (Brewster, MA: Paraclete Press, 2012), 32.

2. *Win a Date with Tad Hamilton!*, directed by Robert Luketic, screenplay by Victor Levin (Glendale, CA: DreamWorks Pictures, 2004).

3. Jared Wilson, "Zack Eswine on the Busy Pastor," *For The Church* podcast, episode 42 (October 16, 2018), https://ftc.co/resource-library /podcast-episodes/episode-042-zack-eswine-on-the-busy-pastor/.

4. Søren Kierkegaard, *Works of Love* (New York: Harper & Row, 1962), 168.

5. Kierkegaard, *Works of Love*, 54.

6. Leon Morris, *Testaments of Love: A Study of Love in the Bible* (Grand Rapids: Eerdmans, 1981), 65.

7. Morris, *Testaments of Love*, 128.

Chapter 3 Make You Feel My Love

1. Dane Ortlund, *Gentle and Lowly: The Heart of Christ for Sinners and Sufferers* (Wheaton: Crossway, 2020), 22.

2. Jonathan Edwards, *Charity and Its Fruits* (Coolidge, AZ: Thornberg Christian Books, 2014), 27.

3. Richard Sibbes, *The Love of Christ* (Carlisle, PA: Banner of Truth, 2011), 199.

4. Dietrich Bonhoeffer, *Life Together* (New York: Harper & Row, 1954), 23.

5. *Punch-Drunk Love*, directed by Paul Thomas Anderson, screenplay by Paul Thomas Anderson (Revolution Studios/New Line Cinema, 2002).

6. Chrysostom, *Love Chapter*, 20.

Chapter 4 Love Is a Battlefield

1. C. S. Lewis, *The Four Loves* (San Diego: Harcourt Brace & Co., 1988), 77.

2. Jerry Bridges, *Respectable Sins* (Colorado Springs: NavPress, 2007), 149.

3. J. R. Miller, *Devotional Hours with the Bible, from the Creation to the Crossing of the Red Sea* (London: Hodder and Stoughton, 1908), 25.

4. Steve Bezner, "On Being Matt Chandler's Roommate," *For The Church* (blog), November 12, 2015, https://ftc.co/resource-library/blog -entries/on-being-matt-chandlers-roommate/. Used by permission.

5. Stephen Altrogge, *The Greener Grass Conspiracy* (Wheaton: Crossway, 2011), 15–16.

Chapter 5 No Ordinary Love

1. Kierkegaard, *Works of Love*, 44.
2. William Law, *A Serious Call to a Devout and Holy Life* (Philadelphia: Westminster, 1955), 105–6.
3. D. A. Carson, *Showing the Spirit: A Theological Exposition of 1 Corinthians 12–14* (Grand Rapids: Baker, 1996), 62.
4. Dallas Willard, *Renovation of the Heart: Putting on the Character of Christ* (Colorado Springs: NavPress, 2002), 104.
5. Francis A. Schaeffer, *True Spirituality* (Wheaton: Tyndale, 1971), 25–26.
6. Richard F. Lovelace, *Dynamics of Spiritual Life: An Evangelical Theology of Renewal* (Downers Grove, IL: InterVarsity, 1979), 85.

Chapter 6 True Love Tends to Forget

1. D. A. Carson, *Love in Hard Places* (Wheaton: Crossway, 2002), 80.
2. Bill Platte, "Survivor of KKK Baptist Church Bombing: 'I Had to Forgive,'" CBS News, May 24, 2013, https://www.cbsnews.com/news/survivor-of-kkk-baptist-church-bombing-i-had-to-forgive/.
3. Charles Spurgeon, "Purging Out the Leaven," *The Metropolitan Tabernacle Pulpit*, vol. 16 (London: Passmore and Alabaster, 1871), 694.
4. Mark Berman, "'I Forgive You.' Relatives of Charleston Church Shooting Victims Address Dylann Roof," *Washington Post*, June 19, 2015, https://www.washingtonpost.com/news/post-nation/wp/2015/06/19/i-forgive-you-relatives-of-charleston-church-victims-address-dylann-roof/.
5. Dustin Waters and Mark Berman, "'You Can't Look at Us': Dylann Roof Formally Sentenced to Death," *Washington Post*, January 11, 2017, https://www.washingtonpost.com/news/post-nation/wp/2017/01/11/families-of-dylann-roofs-victims-offer-him-forgiveness/.
6. Chrysostom, *Love Chapter*, 26–27.
7. John Perkins with Karen Waddles, *One Blood: Parting Words to the Church on Race and Love* (Chicago: Moody, 2018), 105.

Chapter 7 Could You Be Loved?

1. Bob Dylan, "The Groom's Still Waiting at the Altar," *Shot of Love* (Special Rider Music, 1981).
2. Graham Greene, *The End of the Affair* (New York: Penguin, 2004), 1.
3. Morris, *Testaments of Love*, 18.
4. C. S. Lewis, *Surprised by Joy* (London: Geoffrey Bles, 1955), 113.
5. Greene, *End of the Affair*, 159.

6. Greene, *End of the Affair.*

7. John Flavel, *The Method of Grace in the Holy Spirit's Applying to the Souls of Men the Eternal Redemption Contrived by the Father and Accomplished by the Son* (London: Religious Tract Society, 1853), 29.

8. Martin Luther, *The Table Talk of Martin Luther* (Mineola, NY: Dover, 2005), 75.

9. John Bunyan, *Come and Welcome to Jesus Christ* (Carlisle, PA: Banner of Truth, 2011), 150.

10. Samuel Crossman, "My Song Is Love Unknown" (1664), public domain.

Chapter 8 How Deep Is Your Love?

1. Rainer Maria Rilke, *Ahead of All Parting: The Selected Poetry and Prose of Rainer Maria Rilke*, trans. Stephen Mitchell (New York: Modern Library, 1995), 227.

2. Lewis, *The Four Loves*, 65.

Chapter 9 When Love Comes to Town

1. Morris, *Testaments of Love*, 73.

2. John Mayer, "In the Blood," *The Search for Everything* (Reach Music, 2017).

3. *Eternal Sunshine of the Spotless Mind*, directed by Michel Gondry, screenplay by Charlie Kaufman (Universal City, CA: Focus Features, 2004).

4. Timothy Keller with Kathy Keller, *The Meaning of Marriage* (New York: Penguin, 2013), 44.

5. Martin Luther, "Let Your Sins Be Strong," personal letter to Philip Melanchthon, August 1, 1521, https://christian.net/pub/resources/text/wittenberg/luther/letsinsbe.txt.

6. Paul Tripp, "Grace Liberates Our Identity," Paul Tripp Ministries, February 22, 2014, https://assets.speakcdn.com/assets/1804/transcript_liberate_2014.pdf.

Chapter 10 Now That We've Found Love

1. Matthew Barrett, *None Greater: The Undomesticated Attributes of God* (Grand Rapids: Baker Books, 2019), 222.

2. Ross Copperman, Shane McAnally, and Jon Nite, "If I Told You," performed by Darius Rucker, *When Was the Last Time?* (Capitol Records, 2017).

3. Bonhoeffer, *Life Together*, 110–11.

4. Kierkegaard, *Works of Love*, 106–7.

5. C. S. Lewis, *The Voyage of the Dawn Treader* (New York: Harper-Collins, 1994), 109.

6. Lewis, *Voyage of the Dawn Treader*.

7. Edwards, *Charity and Its Fruits*, 14.

Conclusion

1. D. A. Carson, *The Difficult Doctrine of the Love of God* (Wheaton: Crossway, 2000), 62–63, emphasis added.

Jared C. Wilson is assistant professor of pastoral ministry and author in residence at Midwestern Seminary and director of the pastoral training center at Liberty Baptist Church, both in Kansas City, Missouri. He is the author of numerous books, including *The Imperfect Disciple*, *The Prodigal Church* (which won *World Magazine*'s Accessible Theology Book of the Year), and *The Gospel According to Satan*. He is the host of the *For The Church* podcast and cohost of *Christianity Today*'s *The Art of Pastoring* podcast. Jared also blogs regularly at The Gospel Coalition and the For The Church websites, and he speaks at numerous churches and conferences around the world.

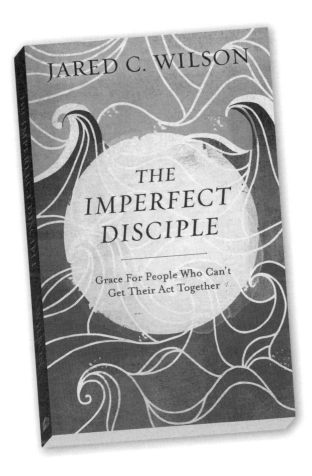

LIKE THIS
BOOK?
Consider sharing it with others!

- Share or mention the book on your social media platforms. Use the hashtag **#LoveMeAnywayBook**.

- Write a book review on your blog or on a retailer site.

- Pick up a copy for friends, family, or anyone who you think would enjoy and be challenged by its message!

- Share this message on Twitter, Facebook, or Instagram: **I loved #LoveMeAnywayBook by @JaredCWilson // @ReadBakerBooks**

- Recommend this book for your church, workplace, book club, or class.

- Follow Baker Books on social media and tell us what you like.

ReadBakerBooks

ReadBakerBooks

ReadBakerBooks